Books by Elie Wiesel

Night
Dawn
The Accident
The Town Beyond the Wall
The Gates of the Forest
The Jews of Silence
Legends of Our Time
A Beggar in Jerusalem
One Generation After
Souls on Fire
The Oath
Ani Maamin
Zalmen, or The Madness of God

Zalmen

or

THE MADNESS OF GOD

Based on a translation from the French
by Nathan Edelman

RANDOM HOUSE · NEW YORK

ZALMEN

or

The Madness of God

Elie Wiesel

ADAPTED FOR THE STAGE
BY MARION WIESEL

Library of Congress Catalog Card Number: 74-24736

ISBN 3-394-49637-x

Manufactured in the United States of America
98765432
First Edition

To those brave Jewish men and women in the U.S.S.R. who broke their silence and ours by declaring themselves free

INTRODUCTION

The year was 1965. On Yom Kippur eve I found myself somewhere in Russia, in a synagogue crowded with people. The air was stifling. The cantor was chanting in drawling, listless tones. All around me were elderly, defeated-looking men. Their eyes were on me, questioning, wondering: Who was I? Where was the stranger from? What message was he bearing? My own eyes were glued to the handsome but seemingly lifeless face of an old man seated on the bimah, facing the congregants. He was praying and sighing as though in a trance. He was the Rabbi. An ancestral, bewildering sadness emanated from his person. He seemed to be living elsewhere, resigned, beyond hope, foundering into a faraway past, even, perhaps, into oblivion.

Suddenly a mad thought crossed my mind: Something is about to happen; any moment now the Rabbi will wake up, shake himself, pound the pulpit and cry out, shout his pain, his rage, his truth. I felt the tension building up inside me; the wait was becoming unbearable. But nothing happened. Nothing interrupted the solemn and disquieting *Kol Nidre* service. The old man remained prisoner of his past, of his fear.

That was when I began to silently implore him. I insisted. I looked only at him, yet I saw nothing but his mask. To me he symbolized the tragic isolation of Russian Jewry humiliated and scarred from the time of the pogroms to the reign of Stalin, enduring a destiny apart, always apart, as though banned from history.

Tall but stooped, the old Rabbi was reciting the customary litanies, oblivious of his surroundings. From time to time his unseeing gaze wandered over the faithful. And all the while I was addressing him soundlessly, pleading with him, my heart beating wildly as though in expectation of a storm long abrewing, a drama about to unfold. I begged the old man: Do something, say something, free yourself tonight and you will enter our people's legend; let the hushed reality buried inside you for so many years explode; speak out, say what oppresses you —one cry, just one, will be enough to bring down the walls that encircle and crush you. My eyes pleaded with him, prodded him. In vain. For him it was too late. He had suffered too much, endured too many ordeals for too many years. He no longer had the strength to imagine himself free.

During the weeks that followed my visit to the Soviet Union, I could not put my encounter with the Rabbi out of my mind. This defeated, beaten old man obsessed my thoughts. His silence lived inside me, his anguish was my torment. Now he, in turn, seemed to be expecting something of me: a gesture, a word, an answer. Could it be that he considered me responsible for his weakness, for his distress? That was when the idea occurred to me to offer him another chance to redeem himself and become the accuser. In my play he seizes that chance, driven by a beadle nicknamed Zalmen the Madman; at last the Rabbi will choose sacrifice.

Conceived as testimony rather than as a work of the

imagination, the play is set in post-Stalin times. The deportees are returning from Siberia, but the terror and silence still dominate the Jewish communities. The tyrant is dead but his law still prevails; the nightmare has not yet lifted. No man—Jew or not—as yet dares to overtly denounce the iniquities and demand his right to freedom and dignity. The victims are still afraid to complain. The scars that cover the body and memory of the Russian Jew have not had time to heal.

Since then, it must be stressed, the situation has changed. In Russia the first to brave their jailers and defy the regime were the Jews. On the eve of Simchath Torah, I saw them dance and sing in front of synagogues, shouting their faith and their pride in Jewish history, celebrating with joy and exultation their inner liberation and loyalty to their past. Before Solzhenitsyn, before Sakharov, they dared proclaim a non-violent rebellion against their oppressors. Well before any other dissidents, they demonstrated their courage by writing letters, signing petitions, calling hunger strikes, occupying government offices. They were the first to set imagination afire—theirs and ours. They were the first to win any victories. They were the ones who gave meaning to the old Rabbi's cries of suffering. They were the ones who allowed hope to ring out across the world.

Are we listening?

The original version of this play, as produced on French radio (directed by René Jentet) and broadcast in two two-hour segments, contained an additional character: Berl, the wise and funny beadle. In the Washington Arena production (directed by Alan Schneider), Zalmen absorbed the role—and the part—of Berl.

CHARACTERS

ZALMEN, a beadle
THE RABBI, spiritual leader
    of the community
THE CHAIRMAN, head of the
    Synagogue Council
Members of the Synagogue
    Council:
    THE DOCTOR
    CHAIM
    SRUL
    SHMUEL
    ZENDER
    MOTKE

THE INSPECTOR, Commissar
    of Jewish Affairs at the
    Ministry of Culture
NINA, the RABBI's daughter
ALEXEY, her husband
MISHA, their son
THE POLICE OFFICIAL
Witnesses:
    AVROM
    FEIGE
THE SECRETARY
A GUARD
THE ACTORS

THE SCENE

The place: A small town somewhere in Russia. The synagogue.
The time: The late fifties—during the so-called Thaw. Stalin is
dead, but his legacy of fear remains.

Act One

As beams of white light strike him full face, ZAL-
MEN *seems startled rather than frightened: we sense
that he is beyond fear. Behind him in the semi-dark-
ness, the old* RABBI, *leaning on his elbows, is studying Talmud, chanting in traditional singsong. From
time to time he stops and sighs.*

ZALMEN
(*Bursts out laughing. He points to the* RABBI)
He never laughs. He just moans and groans—with the
others, for the others. And he calls himself Rabbi . . .
Guide . . . Shepherd . . . Judge . . . Interpreter of the Holy
Word . . . Defender of the Faith. Poor old man—so
weak, so pitiful . . . finding consolation only in tears.

RABBI
Zalmen . . .

ZALMEN
Would you like me to tell you a story? The story of a
holy man who chose the holiest day of the year to face
his entire congregation and declare himself free and
mad? But first—a little warning. The story is beautiful
but not necessarily true. It couldn't really have happened. Not here, not now—it's too late, much too late.
Well, you see . . . Once upon a time, far away, shortly

3

after the death of a tyrant, there was a little town, and in that town there lived a man who no longer knew what it was to be a man. Then one day, one day . . .

RABBI

Zalmen, Zalmen! You're disturbing me!

ZALMEN

Good, Rabbi. I want to disturb you—I want you to do something else, something new.

RABBI

Zalmen, Zalmen. Are you starting again?

ZALMEN

Yes, I'm starting again, and again and again. I'm not afraid of starting. You are. Why? Tell me, Rabbi, why are you afraid?

RABBI

Oh, you and your childish questions . . .

ZALMEN

Never mind if I am a child. I'll probably always be one. Answer me anyway.

RABBI

You want to be told everything—the beginning as well as the end. That is too much for any one person to ask.

ZALMEN

And you, Rabbi? What do you want? What do you really want?

RABBI

Nothing. I am satisfied with what I have, with what I am. The rest is up to God.

ZALMEN

And who tells you this is how God wants you: bowed down, begging for punishment and pardon? Who tells you He wouldn't rather see you strong and proud in spite of your despair?

RABBI

That's blasphemy, Zalmen—and here it is, just a few hours before Yom Kippur.

ZALMEN

What better time to break with past habits—to say things you've never said, to explore the obscure zones of truth. Do you understand what Zalmen is saying?

RABBI

Before Yom Kippur, I cannot lie. Do you want an answer?

ZALMEN

Certainly.

RABBI

You won't be angry? You won't be hurt?

ZALMEN

What difference does it make? I want an answer, Rabbi.

RABBI

Well, the answer is no. I don't understand you. Your allusions, your abrupt changes of mood—I am lost.

ZALMEN

Wonderful, Rabbi! Lose yourself! Shout! Let your call be heard, gather your forces.

RABBI

Keep quiet, Zalmen! You're using words you don't understand!

ZAŁMEN

But you understand them!

RABBI

Enough!

ZALMEN

You're angry, that's good!

RABBI

And you, Zalmen—are insolent!

ZALMEN

You're doing fine. It's a first step, Rabbi! Go on!

RABBI

How dare you offer me advice!

ZALMEN

More, Rabbi, more!

RABBI

Quiet. I order you to be quiet!

ZALMEN

That's how I admire you: threatening, thundering. Let me be the spark and you be the fire. I'll be the clown and you'll be the High Priest.

RABBI

No. No, Zalmen. I will not get angry. You can say anything you like but you will not provoke me. Not today.

ZALMEN

But today may be the day! The day that has been waiting for you and you alone since the beginning of creation. Will you let it slip by, Rabbi? Will you?

RABBI

You are mad, Zalmen. Poor Zalmen . . . But I like you. I don't understand you—but I like you. (*The* CHAIRMAN *knocks*) It must be time for the meeting. Go and get things ready.
> (*Meanwhile, the setting has changed. Now we are in the* shtibel, *the one which also serves as meeting-room for the Council*)

CHAIRMAN

Zalmen . . .

ZALMEN

Oh, Comrade Chairman . . . I didn't hear you.

CHAIRMAN

Is everything ready? Is the Rabbi here? The other members of the Council? It's after ten o'clock and we are late.

ZALMEN

It's my fault, I know, I know.

CHAIRMAN

Keep your confession for services. Go on. Arrange the table . . . the chairs. It's going to be a short day.
(*While* ZALMEN *is running around busily but ineffectually moving chairs, removing prayer-books from the table, etc., some of the Councillors arrive.* ZALMEN *runs from one to the other, pushing one on the way, stepping on another's feet*)

ZALMEN

Your overcoat, Srul Izakovitch.

SRUL

What happened, Zalmen? Why the meeting? Has anything happened?

ZALMEN

What a fine overcoat, Srul Izakovitch. Is it new? It looks it. Expensive?

SHMUEL

This never happened before—a special meeting just a few hours before *Kol Nidre* . . .

ZALMEN

(*Takes his coat and examines it*)

Ah—I envy you, Shmuel Yosifovitch. Such elegance
. . . If I had such a coat, I wouldn't even speak to you.

MOTKE

Zalmen . . . Do you know anything? Why were we
called? What is the reason for all this?

ZALMEN

(*Takes his coat, too. Now he is overloaded*)

Motkele, I don't understand you. You're a tailor. Yet
your coat is worse than the others. Maybe you're not a
tailor?

ZENDER

Two hours, I waited two hours for the tramway. I think
I caught a cold.

CHAIM

Who told you?

ZENDER

A neighbor who has a telephone.

CHAIM

Motke came to tell me. We are neighbors now.

ZENDER

What's the urgency?

ZALMEN

Questions, questions . . . If I had your kind of questions, I'd be a lot happier. Your coat, Doctor. Give me

your coat. (*Buried under the coats, he keeps chattering to himself*) A pleasure to touch . . .

CHAIRMAN

Zalmen . . .

ZALMEN

Not like mine—which doesn't even keep me warm.

CHAIRMAN

Zalmen . . .

ZALMEN

Mine, if it were less ugly, I could say that I wear it just for style. (*He laughs*)

CHAIRMAN

Zalmen, enough.

ZALMEN

Yes, yes, right away, dear Comrade Chairman . . . right away. (*He drops the coats on a chair*) But you, Comrade Chairman, you mustn't stand. Sit down, here, you'll be out of the draft. (*He insists*) Sit down.
(*The* CHAIRMAN *sits down, as do the other Councillors. The* RABBI *enters. All stand up while the old man goes to take his seat at the head of the table*)

RABBI

Good day to you all.

EVERYBODY
(*Speaking at the same time*)
Good day to you too. Good day . . . good year. May
we meet again next year . . . in good health.

RABBI
(*To the* CHAIRMAN)
You called this meeting—? You spoke of an emer-
gency—I am sure you didn't mean . . . an *emergency?*

CHAIRMAN
I did.

SRUL
But why?

ZENDER
When? Who? What?

MOTKE
What's this supposed to mean?

RABBI
I suggest you open the meeting—formally.

CHAIRMAN
The meeting is called to order.
(*Except for the* DOCTOR, *all are past the age of retire-
ment. Most are unshaven, dressed properly but with some
neglect. They appear resigned, expecting nothing more of
themselves. The* DOCTOR *is clean-shaven. Rimless glasses.
Thinning hair. White shirt. Dark tie. Almost elegant. An
intellectual from assimilated surroundings. Why has he*

*joined the congregation? Out of disillusionment? Out of a
yearning for knowledge, for identity? His colleagues do not
understand it; neither does he. They are suspicious of him,
perhaps even envious. He is an outsider*)

ZALMEN

Elye the Reader and Simkhe the Stutterer are missing.

CHAIRMAN

Cowards.

ZALMEN

Perhaps they are sick.

CHAIRMAN

Cowardice *is* a sickness.
(*The* CHAIRMAN: *broad-shouldered, vigorous appearance. Angular face, cold eyes. Massive head, thin lips. His
gestures are abrupt. One senses he is a realistic, practical
man capable of brutality but not of injustice. He looks
gloomy and provoked. He seems to scorn his companions
because they obey him. Does he like them? Probably not. He
likes nothing and nobody, least of all, himself*)

RABBI

Is there something you know that we don't?

CHAIRMAN

They called me to the Ministry yesterday.
(*He pulls out written notes from his pocket*)

RABBI

Well?

12

EVERYBODY

Well? Nu? So? What happened?
(*They look at one another, then at the* RABBI)

RABBI

Aren't *they* pleased? Satisfied?

CHAIRMAN

No.

RABBI

They ought to be—aren't we doing everything . . . ?

CHAIRMAN

Everything? The synagogue has become a club, a mar-
ketplace. People come not to pray but because they have
nothing better to do. They chat, they gossip. They forget
the past too soon. It's a disgrace!

ZENDER

Is that what they told you yesterday?

CHAIRMAN

Yesterday, last week and the week before . . . last
month and the month before. When the Ministry sends
for me in the middle of the night, do you think it's to
offer me a glass of tea?
(*Something in the* CHAIRMAN *'s voice disturbs his colleagues. They listen intently. The tension is growing—and*
ZALMEN *decides that this is the moment to break it*)

ZALMEN
Tea? Did I hear you mention tea? I'll get you tea. As usual. The best, only the best. Comrade Chairman, you like it very strong . . . (*The* CHAIRMAN *remains glum*) Yes, yes, very strong. Three lumps of sugar. As usual.

CHAIRMAN
You are a nuisance. As usual.
(*There is strained laughter*)

ZALMEN
(*Points at the Councillors with his finger*)
Chaim—because of your illness, no sugar. Zender— because of your *health,* no sugar. Zender, how do you feel today?

CHAIRMAN
Get out.
(ZALMEN, *parodying fright, rushes out*)

RABBI
Poor Zalmen, poor Zalmen.

CHAIRMAN
Don't start feeling sorry for him, not now. We have more important things to do. (*He pauses*) We have a problem. (*He pauses again*) Tonight, at services, we shall not be alone. We shall have . . . visitors. Very *special* visitors.

MOTKE
In our synagogue?

14

CHAIM

Tonight?

ZENDER

What visitors?

SRUL

Explain . . .

SHMUEL

Visitors?

MOTKE

From where?

CHAIM

Why tonight?

RABBI
(*Trying to calm them down*)
Shh . . . shh . . . Listen to our Chairman.

CHAIRMAN

They are actors.
(*The excitement grows. Everybody talks at once*)

ZENDER

Comedians?

CHAIM

What's that?

SRUL

They perform . . .

ZENDER

They make people laugh . . .

SHMUEL

At *Kol Nidre?*

CHAIM

Comedians in the synagogue? Never heard of such a
thing—

CHAIRMAN
(*Interrupting*)

They are Jews.
    (*Again, everybody talks excitedly and at the same time*)

SRUL

Jewish actors?

ZENDER

Who are they?

SHMUEL

What do they want?

CHAIM

Who's sending them?

SRUL

For what purpose?

16

ZENDER

To make us laugh on Yom Kippur?

CHAIRMAN

If only you'd stop interrupting all the time.

EVERYBODY

Shh . . . shh . . . Quiet, be quiet. Nu? . . . Quiet.

CHAIRMAN

These are actors from abroad. They're on a tour of the country. Some of them are Jews. Evidently their bus broke down. They'll have to stay here. A day or two. A few of them expressed a wish to attend services in a synagogue. And there's only one here—ours.

(Silence. Anxiety. Dreams. They have been cut off from their people for such a long time, they yearn for a reunion. Only the CHAIRMAN *does not allow himself to show any emotion or hope; hope can be the most dangerous of traps)*

SHMUEL

Jews . . . Jewish actors . . .

MOTKE

Must be important people . . .

SRUL

Unbelievable, I tell you, unbelievable . . .

DOCTOR

Foreign Jews . . .

ZENDER

I had forgotten that they exist . . .

RABBI

Foreign Jews but Jews nevertheless.

CHAIRMAN

(*Harshly*)

Foreigners who happen to be Jewish.

MOTKE

The last time I met a Jew from abroad, it was, let me think, it was . . .

CHAIM

Long ago, so long ago, before my daughter was born . . .

ZENDER

Before my father died . . .

SRUL

In the thirties—I think.

MOTKE

You know, I just realized . . . I had started to think that we, in this forsaken town, were the last Jews on earth.

RABBI

So that's it, then. Tonight we'll see Jews who have come to see us from far away.

CHAIRMAN

Jews who will go back to wherever they came from. We remain.

RABBI

Still, we'll have spent together an hour, a day. What a day! Yom Kippur will be doubly holy, for it will bring us together.

MOTKE

Let's make it a celebration.

SRUL

What an occasion, what an occasion!

CHAIRMAN

An occasion—yes—you're right. An occasion to keep quiet. Do you want a synagogue or not? Listen to me: Don't interfere with our guests—avoid them. Don't embarrass them with complaints, don't try to arouse their pity. Leave them alone.

MOTKE

And I already saw myself celebrating . . .

SRUL

What an occasion!

SHMUEL

Important Jews but still Jews like us—

CHAIRMAN

Stop it. This is no time for nostalgia. If you think we are going to throw ourselves into their arms, you are

wrong. If you expect a sentimental reunion, you are fools. They will be watched and so will we. Is that clear?
(*Standing, the* CHAIRMAN *glares at each one in turn*)

SHMUEL

Comrade Chairman . . .

CHAIRMAN

Is that clear?

SHMUEL

I . . . I have a question.

CHAIRMAN
(*Shouts*)

Is that clear?

SHMUEL
(*Humbled*)

Yes.
(*The* CHAIRMAN *stares at the others*)

CHAIM

Of course.

ZENDER

You know best.

SRUL

No reunion.

MOTKE

Yes, that's clear.

CHAIRMAN
(*To the* DOCTOR)
What about you? Yes—you. (*The* DOCTOR *stares back
but does not open his mouth. The* CHAIRMAN *wants to force
him to yield but changes his mind and turns toward the* RABBI)
And you, Rabbi? You have nothing to say? Not a word?
(*He pauses*) Rabbi!

RABBI
(*Wakes up*)
Oh, what would you like to hear? The things I would
have to say, how can I say them? And who am I to say
them? All I can do is pray—I am the shepherd who
follows his flock.

CHAIRMAN
Then you'll follow me?

RABBI
Naturally.

CHAIRMAN
How far?

RABBI
I've followed you this far—isn't that far enough for
you?

CHAIRMAN
(*Slightly sarcastic*)
You speak little—but well. (*He turns brusquely to the*
DOCTOR *and faces him with suppressed anger*) And you,
Doctor, have you nothing to say? No objections, no

reservations? Not a single comment, not a single word, nothing?

DOCTOR
(*Calm*)
Not a thing.

CHAIRMAN
Of course! Faithful to his ways, his principles, the Doctor says nothing, but very eloquently.

DOCTOR
I have nothing to say.

CHAIRMAN
Because it does not concern you?

DOCTOR
It does.

CHAIRMAN
But not enough to become involved.

DOCTOR
I am involved.

CHAIRMAN
Then say something. Anything. Stop playing the deaf-mute. (*The* DOCTOR *refuses to be provoked, he remains calm*) Oh, well. We are losing time. Go on playing your silly game by yourself, if it amuses you. As for myself, I have a job to do; it will be done. Without you.

DOCTOR

Not entirely without me. I am here.

CHAIRMAN

(*Bangs his fist on the table*)

Stop interrupting me! Now, here are some suggestions: we must isolate the foreigners, carefully choose the
ushers, close off the aisles, the entrances. I want them to
have no contact with our people.

SRUL

But suppose they . . .

CHAIRMAN

If they raise objections, we must tell them that they are
not on stage and not in their own country: here they must
do what we tell them. If you cannot talk to them, I'll do
it.

EVERYBODY

(*Together*)

Yes. No. No problem. Yes, duty first.

(ZALMEN *enters with tea glasses and samovar and places
them on the table before the Councillors*)

ZALMEN

Me too.

CHAIRMAN

(*Taken aback*)

Idiot—you too, what?

ZALMEN

I don't know. Everyone is talking, so I say: me too.

CHAIRMAN

Zalmen!

ZALMEN

I know, I know. I talk too much. Sometimes I stop in the middle of a sentence and ask myself: Zalmen, what on earth are you saying? But since I don't listen to myself, I can't answer.

CHAIRMAN

(*Shrugs scornfully*)

Any other suggestions?

RABBI

One question.

EVERYBODY

Shh . . . shh. The Rabbi . . . listen to the Rabbi.

RABBI

This evening, before *Kol Nidre,* are we not even to invite our guests to take part in the procession?

CHAIRMAN

No.

RABBI

And tomorrow? Are we not to call them to the Torah to read?

CHAIRMAN

No.

RABBI

(*Pleading*)

No one—not a single one? Perhaps it would make
them happy . . .

CHAIRMAN

Let them not be happy. My responsibility is to think of
our well being.

RABBI

When Jews pray together something happens. It will
be difficult to hold back our joy, our feelings. But never
mind . . . I understand, I understand. Tonight, as we pray
to the God of Israel, we shall love all His children—
including our brothers come from afar. Only He will
know.

CHAIRMAN

Only He *should* know.
(*There is an ominous note in his voice. A threat?*)

DOCTOR

Or else . . . Correct?

CHAIRMAN

(*Shrugs angrily*)

The actors are not to leave their seats. And no one is
to go near them.

25

ZENDER

How can we avoid it?

MOTKE

People will want to . . .

SRUL

Ushers, we don't have enough ushers.

CHAIRMAN

The problem was brought up at the Ministry.

SRUL
(*Suspicious*)

What did they suggest?

SHMUEL

Yes, what did they say?

CHAIRMAN

They promised to take care of it.

MOTKE

In what way?

SRUL

A plan . . . they must have a plan.

MOTKE

Do they?

ZENDER

What are they going to do?

CHAIRMAN
They didn't tell me.

DOCTOR
(*Icily*)
I wonder why.

CHAIRMAN
You don't think they tell me everything—or do you?
All they told me is that they'll take care of it. Surely,
they'll find a way.

DOCTOR
I wonder what that way is going to be.
(*The Councillors fall silent.* ZENDER *blows his nose.*
SRUL *lights a cigarette; his hands tremble.* MOTKE *is
making himself small*)

ZALMEN
(*Breaks the tension*)
More tea?

CHAIRMAN
(*Ignores him*)
What's happening to all of you? Lost your tongues all
of a sudden? Like our heroic Doctor?

DOCTOR
Don't get excited. Nobody is blaming you.

CHAIRMAN
(*Stares at him*)
I know you, you and your silences. I see through you:

I disgust you. Why don't you say it once and for all. Speak up! Out with it! Do you hear me?

DOCTOR

I don't hear well when I am shouted at.

CHAIRMAN

Would you rather I kept quiet—like you?

DOCTOR

I didn't say that.

CHAIRMAN

What then?

DOCTOR

Nothing.

CHAIRMAN

(*Menacing*)

Don't push me too far!

RABBI

(*Unhappy*)

Friends, good friends, please—please.

CHAIRMAN

I am asking you a simple question.

RABBI

We are Jews and tonight is Yom Kippur. It's a sin to quarrel. We must help one another—support one another.

CHAIRMAN

This evening something serious could happen. The synagogue will be packed and the foreigners right in the middle. Anything could happen. You know the risks as well as I do. I've recommended a certain line of conduct. And you? What do you recommend? What's your alternative?

DOCTOR

I haven't any.

CHAIRMAN

Is there anything else we should do—anything else we can do?

DOCTOR

I don't think so.

CHAIRMAN

Then you agree with me?

DOCTOR

No.

CHAIRMAN
(*Beside himself, to the others*)
You heard him!

RABBI

He said nothing against you.

CHAIRMAN

It's not what he says that makes my blood boil; it's what he doesn't say. This has been going on for months. Ever since he's arrived in our midst. I do the work and he is my judge—my silent judge! I work, I expose myself, I make enemies and he remains the outsider—the friendly outsider. I commit myself—he doesn't. As a result, everybody curses me, not him. Every misfortune bears my seal, not his. If that's what he wants, that's his business. But I can't tolerate injustice. (*He is on his feet now. Leaning forward, he looks his adversary straight in the eyes*) Let me tell you, right here, in the presence of all: Your detachment is offensive. You do nothing, you say nothing, you expect nothing—do you know what that means? That means that you're not one of us! (*A long hostile silence follows. The* DOCTOR *stiffens in his chair, wants to stand up to refute the charges but changes his mind. The* RABBI *is swaying back and forth sadly, as though studying a particularly obscure passage of Talmud. Suddenly there is a knock at the door. Petrified, all look up. The* RABBI *bites his lips. The* CHAIRMAN's *expression takes on a strange fixity*) Zalmen! Why are you standing there? Go see who it is!

(*Frightened, his beloved teapot in his hand,* ZALMEN *exits, muttering under his breath*)

INSPECTOR
(*Near the entrance*)
I know, you are Zalmen.

ZALMEN
(*Marveling*)
You know me? My name! You really do? Me! My name?

30

INSPECTOR
(*Good-natured*)
But you are famous, Zalmen. The most famous beadle
in the entire area.

ZALMEN
Yes—the only one.

INSPECTOR
Which explains your fame.
(EVERYONE *stands up, including the* RABBI. *They are
troubled and extremely deferential. Perfectly at ease, the*
INSPECTOR *takes off his coat. As* ZALMEN *helps him
clumsily, he drops his precious teapot; luckily it is empty*)

CHAIRMAN
Comrade Inspector, it is an honor . . .

ZALMEN
Me too.

INSPECTOR
You too?

ZALMEN
It's an honor . . .

CHAIRMAN
Pay no attention; he's crazy.

INSPECTOR
You agree, Zalmen?
(*The* INSPECTOR *takes off his hat, remembers Jewish
custom and puts it back on his head*)

31

ZALMEN

Always—Zalmen always agrees.

CHAIRMAN

What an unexpected honor to welcome you here. Allow me, dear Comrade Inspector, to introduce you to the other members of our community.

INSPECTOR

(*Comes closer*)

No ceremony—please. (*Despite his insistence, no one sits down*) Besides, my surprise visit is only semi-official. (*He smiles*) A courtesy call. To get acquainted. I'm not speaking of your esteemed Chairman—he's an old friend. Nor of your Rabbi—we've met before. (*He shakes their hands*) I'm speaking of those among you whom I've not yet had the privilege of meeting. Mind you, you are not strangers to me. Let's see . . . You . . . (*He singles them out and greets them one by one*) you are Yakovlev, Chaim Victorvitch, Pushkin Street 16. Room—let's see—on the first floor, facing the street. Pinsky, Shmuel Yosifovitch—your daughter is still in Moscow. And you, Kazakov, Zender, how is your friendly neighbor? You—Srul Izakovitch, let's see now . . . What were you doing in the old days? Poet, journalist, proofreader, translator, watchman—end of the list. And you—Aaronson, "Motke": tailor, former tailor: unemployed, retired—since when? Six years ago —right? And you—the last—must be Malkin, Yakob Moiseivitch, doctor by profession and angry by vocation. You see? You are all familiar to me. Now it's my turn to introduce myself. Semyonov, Mikhail Lvovitch—of the Ministry of Religious Affairs. My department is— how shall I put it?—the Almighty. My relations with Him

are strictly professional and correct, and like Him I count
on your cooperation to keep them that way.

CHAIRMAN
Count on us, Comrade Inspector, we'll do our best.

INSPECTOR
(*Polite, friendly*)
Thank you, I'm sure you will. But please—do sit
down. I'll take a seat over there, opposite the Rabbi, as
far away as possible.
(*There is laughter*)

CHAIRMAN
Zalmen, an armchair for the Inspector! No, not a chair
—an armchair! You should have thought of that sooner.

ZALMEN
How could I have imagined that . . .
(ZALMEN *runs into the other room and brings in a heavy
armchair*)

CHAIRMAN
Put it down—move!

INSPECTOR
Thank you, Comrade Beadle.

CHAIRMAN
Thank you, Zalmen.

ZALMEN
Tea? I am also famous for my tea . . .

INSPECTOR

Oh, I know: you have many talents.

CHAIRMAN

Except one—how to hold his tongue.
(INSPECTOR: *in his forties. Open face, mocking eyes. Thick, reddish hair. Correctly dressed. Hearty laugh. He treats the Councillors not as enemies but as inexperienced citizens whom he must guide to prevent them from making foolish mistakes*)

INSPECTOR

I'm terribly busy these days. Your God has arranged things badly—too many holidays in one month. And your Moses was not only a poor speaker, he was a terrible planning commissar.

MOTKE

Not our fault, Comrade Inspector. That's the Bible. We had nothing to do with it.

CHAIRMAN

Thank you, Motke. The Inspector knows the Bible as well as you do—if not better.

MOTKE

I didn't mean to imply . . .

INSPECTOR

Let's not exaggerate. Naturally, I have read the Bible, a few pages here and there, like everybody else, out of curiosity, as part of my professional training. And by the way, I find it an amusing book, rather interesting and *even* well written, but—forgive me—terribly outdated.

34

RABBI

For us . . . it is eternal . . . and sacred.

INSPECTOR

Ah yes, the Holy Bible—and so on. But isn't holiness itself outdated? Today's saints spend their nights in factories and laboratories rather than in churches and synagogues. Like their religious predecessors, they too hope to get closer to heaven . . . only *they* are succeeding.

DOCTOR

Perhaps we should redefine our terms. Let us say a saint is someone who does not succeed.

CHAIRMAN

Our Doctor loves contradictions . . .
   (*There is laughter*)

INSPECTOR

And he has answers for everything?

CHAIRMAN

He? Answers? He has nothing but questions—and when he doesn't, he wants to know why not.

DOCTOR

Our Chairman has no taste for questions.

ZALMEN

Here is your tea, esteemed Comrade Inspector. Tea is an answer which no question can resist. (*To the* DOCTOR) You too, Doctor—have some more tea; it'll do you good.

DOCTOR

Thanks for the prescription.

INSPECTOR

Well done, Zalmen. You, for one, know how to handle him. You should have been a doctor yourself.

ZALMEN

God forbid! Then who would be the beadle?

INSPECTOR

And you, Rabbi? Which side are you on? The questions or the answers?

RABBI

I am on the side of prayer.

INSPECTOR

If I understand you correctly, between the Chairman and the Doctor, you very wisely choose . . . Zalmen?

RABBI

I choose prayer.

INSPECTOR

What *is* prayer: question or answer?

RABBI

Both. Question for whoever believes he has found an answer. Answer for whoever struggles with the question.

INSPECTOR

Now we are getting into theology—I am lost.

RABBI

I pray in order not to be lost.

INSPECTOR

(*Feigning annoyance*)

Come, Rabbi. Try to keep it simple. I'd really like to know what prayer is.

RABBI

It is neither question nor answer. Or rather, it is both. Or better yet, it is that which links the one to the other.

INSPECTOR

I give up. I am no match for you.

RABBI

Only in matters of prayer, Comrade Inspector, only in matters of prayer.

INSPECTOR

Is there anything else that matters—to you? (*He becomes serious again*) Let's turn to some earthly matters: Plans for tonight and tomorrow.

CHAIRMAN

Everything will be all right. No incidents, no surprises. You can count on us.

INSPECTOR

Excellent. After all, it's in your own interest to preserve the purely religious character of your holidays. (*There is general acquiescence*) What steps have you considered?

CHAIRMAN

Complete isolation of the visitors.

CHAIM

A security cordon.

ZENDER

Strict supervision.

SRUL

We may be short of ushers.

MOTKE

We'll manage.

SHMUEL

No one will get close to them . . .

CHAIM

We'll see to it.

RABBI

Everything will be all right.

CHAIRMAN

How many are they?

INSPECTOR

The actors? Twelve. Four are Jewish. But even the others wish to attend your services. One of them speaks a little Russian. A crazy world: Christians want to hear *Kol Nidre*, a prayer which, if I am not mistaken, was sanctified by Jews who refused to become Christians.

38

CHAIRMAN
Yes, indeed, a crazy world.

INSPECTOR
Don't forget—they're our guests. As such, they're to be treated with courtesy and respect.

CHAIRMAN
You have my word.

INSPECTOR
Personally, I trust you. Still, we can never be cautious enough. Don't be offended, but to forestall and discourage any . . . shall we say . . . "unfortunate incidents," we have decided to offer you more concrete assistance. On a temporary basis, of course. Tonight and tomorrow we'll have our own people in the synagogue. (*He pauses —to see the effect*) Don't worry, comrades. They won't bother you. They won't even pray: they will not be competition.

CHAIRMAN
(*Dissatisfied*)
But they *will* attract attention . . .

INSPECTOR
Certainly.

CHAIRMAN
You want them to attract attention?

INSPECTOR
Precisely. Their presence will serve as a deterrent. (*He scrutinizes them*) Any objections?

CHAIRMAN
None.

SRUL
Objections? No objections.

MOTKE
No, no—what objections could there be?

RABBI
(*Somber*)
You'll see, everything will be all right, everything will
be all right.

INSPECTOR
We are doing all this for your own good. (*They all nod
in agreement*) I'm expected at the office. I'm going to meet
these actors. And they will talk to me about God and
Jews. What a crazy world, God takes up all my time. (*He
gets up. All follow suit*) Well, I feel we understand one
another. Thank you for your attention, (*To the* DOCTOR)
Thank you for your questions. (*To the* CHAIRMAN) And
for your answers. (*To the* RABBI) And for your prayers.
To all, goodbye.

EVERYBODY
Goodbye, goodbye, goodbye, Comrade Inspector.

ZALMEN
Your coat, your coat . . . Here it is. I put it away
separately.

RABBI

Everything will be all right. (*He sighs*) Dear God, let everything be all right.

(*The* INSPECTOR *exits, followed by the* CHAIRMAN *and* ZALMEN. *The others remain like statues for a long moment.* ZALMEN *reappears, breathing into his cold hands*)

ZENDER

Actors . . .

CHAIM

Jewish actors . . .

SRUL

Jewish actors from abroad . . .

SHMUEL

I wonder . . .

ZENDER

What's there to wonder about? Actors are actors.

SRUL

Actors are people—and people are people.

CHAIRMAN

The meeting is over. We can go now.

CHAIM

We should go now. It's late.

MOTKE

It's almost time to come back for *Kol Nidre.*

RABBI

May God bless you with a good year.

EVERYBODY

Have a good year, Rabbi . . . a healthy year.

RABBI

May God make us live and survive another year.

ZALMEN

I'll bring you your lunch in just a moment . . . Did I
tell you your daughter is coming to see you? I'm sure
she'll bring something.

(*All exit except the* DOCTOR, *who addresses the* CHAIR-
MAN *at the door*)

DOCTOR

Congratulations! Official security agents in the synagogue! Your own informers no longer suffice!

CHAIRMAN

Aren't you the talkative one all of a sudden!

DOCTOR

Was that *your* idea?

CHAIRMAN
(*Hissing*)

It pleases you to think that, doesn't it? Well, it wasn't.
If I want to arrange something, I do it openly.

DOCTOR

This was not your idea?

42

CHAIRMAN

I was as surprised as you. But then—let them come this evening, or any evening. Let them watch—we have nothing to hide, nothing to fear.

DOCTOR

Nothing?

CHAIRMAN

Let them come so that we may have nothing to fear. Let our people learn once and for all that patience is a condition of survival, let them learn . . .

DOCTOR

. . . to suffer in silence.

CHAIRMAN

Precisely! In silence! In silence! We live in difficult times! The Georgian is dead, and things are getting better but—why hurry too fast? Why risk everything by provoking the authorities? Where is all this going to lead us?

DOCTOR

Us? You include me?

CHAIRMAN

No, not you. You are not one of us. I never did understand what in the world you were doing in a synagogue!

DOCTOR

I like to be with Jews. We are on the same side. Whether you like it or not, we belong to the same people.

43

CHAIRMAN

But you hate me!

DOCTOR

I don't hate you. Sometimes I admire you, sometimes I feel sorry for you. But most of the time I am angry with you—though never as much as with myself.

CHAIRMAN

Then—what would you do in my place?

DOCTOR

I've no idea. The same as you perhaps.

CHAIRMAN

Meaning?

DOCTOR

Perhaps one can do nothing more.

CHAIRMAN

Go on.

DOCTOR

Perhaps one *must* do nothing more.

CHAIRMAN

Yes?

DOCTOR

I said perhaps. That's as far as I will go.

44

CHAIRMAN

That's far enough for me. You know what I mean. You are neither stupid nor naïve. We have managed to survive innumerable persecutions over the centuries. How did we do it? We learned to wait, to exercise restraint. Waiting was a necessity for us and we turned it into an art. That required sacrificing certain relationships, certain rituals—so what? We had no choice. Don't you think I too could give up, choose the easy way out and resign? Would that solve the problem? Surely not. Therefore, I say we must accept and endure and—don't be shocked—collaborate. Or at least, play the game of collaboration.

DOCTOR

That's your game and you play it well—with plenty of conviction.

CHAIRMAN

Why not? I believe in it. It's the only possible way. Not to act with haste, not to remind the authorities thirty times a month and three times a day that forty years after the Revolution the Jewish question remains unsolved and burning . . .

DOCTOR

Because . . . it is not?

CHAIRMAN

Of course it is! But why talk about it? Why stir up trouble? In order to survive, we must bend and let the storm pass. There's the lesson Jewish history has given us!

DOCTOR

I've never studied Jewish history.

CHAIRMAN

I have. And believe me—my method is valid. It's been
tested so many times—over and over again. So why do
you want to fight me? Why are you my enemy?

DOCTOR

I am not your enemy and I fight you so little—and so
poorly.

CHAIRMAN

Don't tell me you're my friend!

DOCTOR

I am not. And I will tell you why. It is true I don't know
our Jews, but I feel compassion for them. You don't. You
don't even like them. All these people who fear you,
who, even at services, don't dare reveal their real names
to their neighbors—you have no love for them, no compassion! You pretend to be thinking of the future, of the
abstract Jew of the year 2000, and for his sake you
manipulate the Jew of today, as if he were an object—
some kind of tool!

CHAIRMAN

(*Red with anger*)

Is that what you really think?

DOCTOR

You allow yourself to terrorize these people, to
smother their spirit—yet you are playing a game whose

46

rules have been set by others. Do you hope to become the instrument of our survival? Poor fool—you are nothing but a puppet whose strings are pulled by others.

CHAIRMAN
(*Shaken*)
You really believe that?

DOCTOR
Of course I do. Your intentions may be good but that's no excuse. Our community is dying and you don't share its pain, its anguish.

CHAIRMAN
You're saying these things just to insult me, to hurt me.

DOCTOR
You wanted to hear the truth—you've heard it. Anyway, I am not alone in feeling that way about you. We all do. In our eyes you are an instrument—and while instruments feel no pain, neither do they inspire affection. You are feared and despised.
(*The* CHAIRMAN *and the* DOCTOR *stare at one another. Standing in the doorway, the* RABBI *and* ZALMEN, *aghast, don't dare interfere or even come forward*)

CHAIRMAN
If one of us deserves to be despised, it is you. Where were you all these years? Where were you when the danger was real? When we were afraid of our own shadows. You just arrived and already you are judging and condemning, and you do nothing else. I at least try to

47

help certain people in certain situations—you do nothing! I may be unable to exorcise evil or conquer it, but at least I try to lessen its impact. But you, what do you do?

DOCTOR

What?

CHAIRMAN

You set yourself up as defender of Jews. You make me laugh. What do you know about us—when have you lived with us? What are you doing for us? You don't even inspire us . . .

DOCTOR

Go on.

CHAIRMAN

Tonight, for example, would you encourage us to overturn the barriers? To run to our visitors—our brothers from abroad—and embrace them? Would you yourself go and see them . . . and talk to them . . . and open your heart to them? Would you be willing to take risks? Oh no! You look and you judge, you observe and you condemn—and you let others decide. You want others to do the work, so that your conscience may remain clean. Your conscience, your precious conscience.

DOCTOR

What else?

48

CHAIRMAN

As for compassion . . . and suffering . . . (*He sighs*) What do you know about suffering? Oh yes, you took part in the war, saw the mass graves, met the survivors—but that's not enough. That's not enough, I tell you. I was in Leningrad—I was there during the siege, from beginning to end. And I say to you that what you know about suffering is nothing.

Suffering, true suffering, eludes memory and words. Suffering, true suffering, is watching death— dark, cunning death—drawing close to children too weak to cry. Children you love. Your own. With a piece of bread, a spoonful of soup, a bit of warmth you could chase it away, but your hands are empty, you have nothing left to offer. And you want to howl, to shout at the top of your lungs, to tear out your hair and your eyes. But you do nothing. You don't even feel guilty. Just sad. Terribly sad. And stupidly useless. You feel idle and empty—empty of faith. Forlorn. Abandoned even by imagination. A dull, heavy animal. Deaf and blind. And alone. Terribly alone . . . (*Suddenly he notices the* RABBI *and* ZALMEN. *He takes hold of himself, becomes arrogant once more*) Anyway, what good is it to talk to you! Go away! Get out of my sight!

(*The* CHAIRMAN *brushes past the* RABBI *without greeting him. The* DOCTOR *is about to follow but the* RABBI *holds him back*)

RABBI
(*Gently*)

Please don't go yet.

DOCTOR

It's getting late.

RABBI

Stay a while. Please. (*He sits down. The* DOCTOR *remains standing.* ZALMEN *leaves discreetly*) He has suffered. Too much perhaps for one man.

DOCTOR

I know.

RABBI

His wife. Two small children. Dead. Of hunger. In the street. There he was. Suddenly alone.

DOCTOR

Suffering is no excuse.

RABBI
(*Smiles sadly*)

Isn't it?

DOCTOR

The excuse is too simple, too convenient.

RABBI

Do you know any excuse that isn't?

DOCTOR

I am not looking for excuses.

RABBI

What are you looking for?

DOCTOR

Meaning.

RABBI

Have you found it?

DOCTOR

Not yet. (*He pauses*) But one thing I know already: the experience of suffering is not an end—an end in itself—only a beginning.

RABBI

A beginning of what?

DOCTOR

I don't know. I am still at the beginning. I am still searching.

RABBI

And what if I were to tell you that certain quests can be too burdensome for one man?

DOCTOR

I would continue nevertheless.

RABBI

And he accuses *you* of weakness!

DOCTOR

Maybe he is right. I'm no hero. There is no virtue in seeking.

Still it is painful.

There is no virtue in accepting pain.

You too have suffered . . .

A little more, a little less . . . like everyone else of my generation. When all is said and done, it adds up to nothing.

Nothing?

Almost nothing. And then—it all seems so far away.

(After a pause)
The Chairman is probably right: what matters is to survive.

I know the formula: the dead are dead and the living owe it to themselves to go on living. Except that I have seen too many corpses. Corpses all look alike. It was as though one Jew, always the same, had been killed six million times by one murderer, always the same. (*He pauses*) And then I say to myself: You have been spared. And you don't even know why. And I am overcome with rage. And shame.

RABBI

You are alive—be grateful for that. To be a Jew means to choose life.

DOCTOR

You are talking to a doctor, Rabbi. Do you really think man can choose to live?

RABBI

It's all a question of where you place the accent. God requires of man not that he live, but that he choose to live. What matters is to choose—at the risk of being defeated.

DOCTOR

And then . . . we die.

RABBI

Death comes only later; it does not affect the choice itself.

DOCTOR

And you, Rabbi—are you still making choices?

RABBI

(*Hesitates*)

I . . . I used to. Now I am too old.

DOCTOR

I envy you. I never had an alternative. I didn't choose to live any more than the others chose to be killed. All this is so confusing . . . I don't understand. I am a Jew, though I don't really know what it means to be Jewish.

My parents were fervent . . . non-believers. I am not observant, not religious. I believe in man—in man alone. My wife isn't Jewish, neither is our daughter. I find it difficult to talk with them. I often feel like a stranger in my own house. Is that why I joined the synagogue? To be among my own people? Oh, I don't know. Perhaps the Chairman is right: I am here for selfish reasons. It is cold out there; no friends to count on . . . under suspicion, unwanted always. At the front they used to tell *me* —an officer with three citations—jokes about Jewish cowards. They used to tell *me* that Jews buy their medals at the market in Tashkent. Sometimes I wish I could go somewhere else, somewhere far away, somewhere where I would feel I belong. But I know of no such place, so I come here.

RABBI

I feel sad for you.

DOCTOR

I am sorry.

RABBI

Don't be. I welcome this sadness. (*He pauses*) I would have liked you to be my ally. Helping me to make Jews understand their suffering and overcome it by turning it into joy and song.

DOCTOR

I'm no miracle-maker, Rabbi.

RABBI

No? My friend, then how can you be a Jew?
(*The exchange between the* RABBI *and the* DOCTOR *is
interrupted by the appearance of* ZALMEN)

ZALMEN

Forgive me, Rabbi . . . it *is* getting late.

DOCTOR

Yes . . . Have a good year, Rabbi. You too, Zalmen.

RABBI

Have a peaceful year, my friend.

DOCTOR

Peaceful . . .
(*The* DOCTOR *exits*)

ZALMEN

Your daughter will be here any minute . . . You'll have
lunch.

RABBI

I'm not hungry.

ZALMEN

You must eat. You cannot fast two days in a row.

RABBI

I'm not hungry, Zalmen.

ZALMEN

You need strength, Rabbi.

55

RABBI

How do you know what I need?

ZALMEN

I know what *I* need, Rabbi. I need to know you strong.

RABBI

Zalmen, Zalmen, my *poor* Zalmen.

ZALMEN

Why do you feel sorry for me? Because I want you to
enter your dream? And choose martyrdom? Because I
want you to become mad?

RABBI

Quiet, Zalmen! Be quiet!

ZALMEN

Break the chains, Rabbi! Let your anger explode! This
is your chance. A chance offered by God! Don't let it slip
away!

RABBI

Enough, Zalmen! You won't succeed: I refuse to get
angry. Not today. You may push my patience to its limit
—but I will not be provoked. I will not listen.

ZALMEN

Yes, you will. You *are* listening.

RABBI

No, no, Zalmen—I won't listen to you. Not today.

56

ZALMEN
(*Softly*)
When my mother died, my father took me to his *rebbe*
for Yom Kippur and said to me: he's a great man, an
illustrious man; hitch your prayers onto his. I imagined
him powerful, invincible. That night, before *Kol Nidre,*
I saw him—a sickly, frail old man, hardly able to stand
on his feet, barely breathing. Yet, at the hour of prayer,
he shed his weakness, his age; he was a fighter once more,
ready, for the good of his community, to do battle with
God Himself. He clenched his fists and became the powerful and vocal spokesman of that community; and the
will of every man present converged in his. You can be
that *rebbe!*

RABBI
Your *rebbe* took his strength from his Jews. From mine
I take nothing but anguish.

ZALMEN
Try, Rabbi. I'll help you—we'll all help you.

RABBI
Too late, Zalmen . . . too late.
(ZALMEN *shakes his head. The* RABBI, *deep in thought,*
does not hear the knocking at the door. A woman and her
son enter noiselessly, as if into a sickroom. ZALMEN *exits*
still shaking his head. NINA: *plump but beautiful, her*
long hair tied into a knot. MISHA: *a schoolboy, shy,*
curious, well-mannered. There are books under his arm.
NINA *waits a moment before making her presence known*)

57

NINA

Hello, Father. (*The* RABBI *seems not to hear her. He does not react*) Father, you look pale . . . so pale. Are you all right?

RABBI
(*In a daze*)

Oh, it's you. I was not expecting you any more. No—that's not true. I was waiting for you.

NINA

You knew I would come, Father.

RABBI

You mean I should have known? (NINA *nods*) Thank you, Nina.

NINA

I'm late—I'm sorry. I had to go get Misha from school.

RABBI
(*Starts*)

Misha? Misha is here? Misha, where are you?

MISHA

Good morning, Dyedushka.

RABBI

Where are you, Misha? Let me see you. Come closer, son. Closer. So, there you are. Let me look at you. How you've grown, Mishinka. Let me bless you. You come so seldom . . .

58

NINA

We can't stay very long.

RABBI

So seldom and for so short a while.

NINA

(*Embarrassed*)

It's not his fault, Father. School takes all his time. You can't imagine . . . It's inhuman what they expect of children today.

MISHA

It's not all that hard, Dyedushka. Mother exaggerates. You know her . . .

RABBI

Yes, I know her, son.

MISHA

Did she tell you I skipped a year?

RABBI

I'm proud of you. So is your mother.

NINA

He works too much—it worries me; he's so frail. He doesn't eat, he doesn't sleep. He's always buried in his books.

RABBI

Exactly what my mother used to say about me. Only the books are not the same.

(*The* RABBI *thumbs through* MISHA*'s books*)

MISHA

If I continue to do well, Papa says . . .

NINA

(*Nervous*)

We must go. We just came for a minute.

MISHA

I could go to the university in Moscow—that's what Papa says.

RABBI

Yes, yes—you will go far. But what do you want to be when you grow up?

MISHA

A scientist.

NINA

He just loves mathematics . . . physics.

RABBI

Yes, yes—you will become a great scientist if they let you. People will recognize you in the street. You will be famous. And then—will you come to see me more often? And stay longer?

NINA

Father, he still has a long way to go.

MISHA

First—I have to finish gymnasium.

NINA

Five years, four—if he doesn't get lazy.

MISHA

Mamushka . . . please . . .

RABBI

Four years . . . that's a long time. (*He smiles affectionately, sadly*) All right. I'll wait . . . if I can.

NINA

(*Catches the implication*)

He'll come to see you . . . soon. But now we must leave. We'll come back another time . . . as soon as possible.

RABBI

And your husband will let him? He won't worry about my evil influence?

NINA

You are too harsh, Father. In his own way, Alexey is fond of you.

RABBI

(*Laconic*)

I would not have guessed it.

That's because you refuse to understand him. Still, it's true—he is fond of you—even though you are too harsh with him.

MISHA

I'm very fond of you.

RABBI

I know, son, I know. Maybe I *am* too harsh with your father. After all, he did allow you both to come here today—even though it's Yom Kippur eve. He wasn't happy about it last year . . . (*He notices* NINA*'s expression change*) He *did* allow you to come, didn't he?

NINA
(*Mumbles*)
Of course . . . Naturally . . . But—we must leave. Now we must go. We've already overstayed. Come, Misha . . .

RABBI

Did he permit you to come: yes or no?

NINA

Don't get upset, Father.

RABBI

Yes or no?

NINA

You are getting all upset for nothing.

RABBI

Yes or no?

NINA

(*Whispers*)

Well, no . . . not exactly. (*She pauses—the* RABBI *understands*) It's so unimportant, Father . . . believe me. Anyway, we are here. Misha and I. The rest doesn't matter.

MISHA

I'll miss school this afternoon. But don't worry, I'll catch up.

RABBI

(*Not listening, following his own thoughts*)

So, I was right. Your husband doesn't know. You didn't tell him. Were you afraid or ashamed to tell him?

NINA

Try to understand him, Father. Don't be against him. Please. His position is not an easy one. He must be careful. People talk . . .

RABBI

And what do they say?

NINA

Nothing . . . nothing. Nothing specific, nothing unpleasant. But you know what I mean.

RABBI

Then why did you come? Why do you jeopardize your husband's career?

63

NINA

Father, don't talk to me like that, I beg of you—not in that tone of voice!

RABBI

How do you want me to talk to you? Anyway, my tone of voice has never stopped you from doing what you wanted to do!

NINA
(*On the verge of tears*)
Father, I beg you . . . I have enough problems.

RABBI
(*Somber*)

So do I.

NINA

Why not accept things as they are? Aren't you happy to see us—to see Misha? Why kill your joy, and ours? Why not accept this moment for what it is? Why not be more generous? After all, tomorrow is Yom Kippur.

RABBI
(*Ironic*)

So you do remember . . .

NINA
(*Smiles*)

I am still a rabbi's daughter.

RABBI
(*Softened*)
Tell me, Misha, what *is* Yom Kippur?

MISHA
A holiday . . . I think. An important holiday—a Jewish
holiday.

RABBI
What sort of holiday?

MISHA
For old people.

RABBI
Like me?

MISHA
(*Hesitates*)
Yes—like you, Dyedushka.

RABBI
And these old people—what do they do on Yom Kippur?

MISHA
They get together in the synagogue.

RABBI
And what do they do there?

MISHA
They pray . . . I think. And they cry.

65

RABBI

Why do they cry?

MISHA

I don't know, Dyedushka. Maybe because . . . they're old.

RABBI

And you, Mishinka, when you are old—will you also come?

NINA

Father!

MISHA

I don't know. I never thought about it.

RABBI

And what if I asked you to come with me . . . tomorrow? Or . . . tonight?

NINA

Father!

MISHA

I can't, Dyedushka. I have homework tonight . . . and tomorrow I have school. Besides, I'm not old yet!

RABBI

You will be one day. And I won't be here to put this question to you—so I put it to you now: When you're old, will you go to synagogue?

MISHA

I don't know, Dyedushka. I don't know yet . . .

RABBI

Will you think about it?

NINA

Father, Misha is only a child!

RABBI

How old are you, son?

MISHA

Twelve.

RABBI

One year until your bar mitzvah . . .
(MISHA *looks questioningly at his mother*)

NINA

(*With growing uneasiness*)
We really have to go . . .

RABBI

You don't like to hear me talk about such things, do
you, my daughter?

NINA

Please—don't ask too much of us. Out of considera-
tion for you, in order not to hurt your feelings, and
because you were so insistent—we agreed to have Misha
circumcised. But there is a limit. Put yourself in our
place . . .

RABBI

I see. No bar mitzvah for Misha. Your son. My grandson—my only one. The descendant of the celebrated Reb
Aizik'l, my father, of whom it was said that he rushed
through life without ever taking his eyes off the Torah.
No bar mitzvah for his child . . . (*The* RABBI *sighs*)

NINA

Father, please . . .

RABBI

But then—what's the difference? It's nothing but a
symbolic gesture, full of meaning, of promise too, if one
is Jewish before and after—but in itself, devoid of signifi-
cance. Even if Misha went through his bar mitzvah, how
would that change anything? Ceremony or not, it is all
the same.

NINA

You refuse to understand, Father, how difficult it is for
a boy today to grow up in your image.

RABBI

I remember the first lesson my father taught me. I was
three—perhaps less. The first time I said *Shma Israel.*
When a Jewish child reaches the age of three, it becomes
his father's duty to teach him this affirmation of our faith
. . . that the God of Israel is our God and that He is One.

NINA

Father! Your father was a pious Jew—Misha's is not!

MISHA

I don't understand . . .

RABBI

Neither do I, son, neither do I. Here you are. Here
is your mother. Here am I. And tomorrow is Yom Kippur, the most holy, the most important day of the year
and yet . . . in all this there is something I do not understand, something which escapes me, something which
breaks my heart.

(*The* RABBI*'s head is bowed. There is a long silence,
broken only when the door opens with a shattering bang.*
ALEXEY ADAMOV *enters. Thirtyish, tall, energetic,
tense. Like a man robbed, he has come to claim what
belongs to him and leave as quickly as possible.* NINA*'s
face reflects anguish and* MISHA*'s amazement. The*
RABBI *looks at his son-in-law with sadness*)

NINA

Alexey . . .

ALEXEY

I knew it! I knew you'd take him out of school.

NINA

Forgive me . . .

ALEXEY

I don't like those words. Not on your lips or mine.

NINA

I had to come here . . . with Misha. He just had to wish
his grandfather a happy new year . . . Father's not very
young any more.

ALEXEY

You just had to come.

RABBI
(*Almost serene*)
Good afternoon, Alexey.

ALEXEY
(*Sarcastic*)
Good afternoon? You mean happy new year. Why not
wish me a good fast while you're at it?

RABBI

Strange . . . you are a Jew. I am a Jew. Yet—between
us, there is an abyss.

ALEXEY

Who am I to contradict you . . .

NINA

Alexey! Father is more than twice your age!

RABBI

Let him, Nina. Your husband does not respect age. In
fact, he rejects it. I am old—therefore I represent the
past; and the past must be repudiated.

ALEXEY

Only yours.

RABBI

We share the same past, Alexey—and this too I find strange. You resent it while I assume it. You may laugh, but sometimes I feel three thousand years old—and to me, that is a great comfort.

ALEXEY

A fine comfort! With its outlandish rituals, its senseless superstitions, your past is a burden—a dead weight that stops you from moving forward.

RABBI

A fallacy, Alexey. I move forward—just like you and the others like you—though a little more slowly. There are advantages to that. It enables me to look about me, to admire twilight as it draws closer, and also, with a little luck, to befriend others who like myself are looking for the source and know where it can be found no matter how inaccessible it seems.

ALEXEY

And to reach that source, you must go back three thousand years?

RABBI

At times.

ALEXEY

It's tiring to walk three thousand years.

RABBI

Very tiring—more than you think.

ALEXEY

Well, once again I tell you I have no use for that kind of journey, that kind of weariness. When will you finally understand? I want no part of it.
> (*Troubled by the hostility between the two men,* MISHA *picks up a Hebrew book lying on the bench and thumbs through it.* ALEXEY *snaps it shut in his face and pushes him toward the exit.* MISHA *resists but lets himself be pushed.* ALEXEY *is leaving. He is stopped by the* RABBI)

RABBI

What are you afraid of, Alexey? Our past? Does it frighten you that much?

ALEXEY

Nothing frightens me. But since the past is a burden, I cast it off.

RABBI

(*Unhappy*)

But why, Alexey, why?

ALEXEY

(*Leaves* MISHA *at the door and returns to face the* RABBI)
I've told you a thousand times, I will tell you again. I don't want my son to grow up a stranger in his own country—with his back to the wall, alienated from society. I want him to be a normal, proud, healthy child without complexes or prejudices! I don't want him to go around obsessed by the idea that he's different, better or worse than others!

NINA

Alexey . . . Father . . . Don't quarrel—not again.
Please, please!

RABBI

Let him speak, daughter. It's not often I have a chance
to talk things out with your husband.

ALEXEY

What's the use? You don't listen! You are deaf!

RABBI

Compliment for compliment: if I am deaf, you are
blind.

ALEXEY

Blind—me? It is you who are blind. Deaf and blind.
Deaf to our ideas, blind to reality!

RABBI

I see very well, and what I see is not always very
encouraging.

ALEXEY

No. You don't see well because you are looking with
Jewish eyes!

RABBI

But I am a Jew, Alexey! As you are yourself. That too
worries me.

ALEXEY

Don't worry about me!

RABBI

Not about you. About Misha. And still more about his son: Will *he* be a Jew?

ALEXEY

He will be a man—that's enough for me.

RABBI

Then a Jew, according to you, is not a man?

ALEXEY

Not like other men. You said so yourself. A Jew walks differently—bent over—like a thief, a beggar, an aimless wanderer!

RABBI

If the backs of Jews are bent, whose fault is it?

ALEXEY

Their own. Let them stand up straight! How many times must I tell you that I will not allow my son to live in suffering, in humiliation, a captive of memories and ghosts, forever on guard, forever oppressed by sadness! I don't want him to suspect an enemy in every passer-by. I don't want him trailed by legions of shadows! Do you hear me? I don't want him to inherit the tears of our fathers—I want him to forget.

RABBI

(*Overwhelmed*)

To forget—you want him to forget . . .

ALEXEY

Yes—*yes.*

MISHA

I don't understand. Papa . . . Dyedushka . . . I don't understand.
(*The men ignore* MISHA*'s interruptions*)

NINA

You're too young to understand.

MISHA

But, Mamushka, I . . . I want to . . .

NINA
(*Trying to contain her sobs*)
Quiet, Misha, be quiet.

RABBI

To forget, you want him to forget! Then you have made your choice in his name!

ALEXEY

Exactly. I consider it my right—my duty! You want to preserve his past—I want to save his future!

RABBI
(*Crushed*)
I see. Another branch broken from the living tree of Israel. That's what you want. To smother the spark. Silence the song. Is that really what you want? Tell me!

ALEXEY

Much more and much less. I don't think in those terms.
You're thinking of an entire people; I am concerned with
my son. I shall break the chain that links him to misfortune. My father suffered as a Jew, and so did his, and so
did my great-grandfather and his father before him. How
long do you want this to go on? I say: Enough, enough!
It must stop. Once and for all. With my son—it will!

NINA

Father, don't answer! Don't argue! Don't listen to him.
Try to understand us. At least—try!

RABBI

I understand, oh yes, I understand. You would like
there to be no more Jews in this land—you would like
the Jew in me to die with me.

NINA

Don't say those things, Father. We are not talking
about you! And why do you speak of dying?

ALEXEY

That's enough! I can't stand sentimentality! All this is
leading us nowhere—nowhere! Let's go! Let's go!
    (ALEXEY *dashes out*)

NINA

Goodbye, Father. Take good care of yourself. Have an
easy fast . . . and a happy new year.
    (NINA *follows her husband*)

MISHA
(*At the door*)
Goodbye, Dyedushka.

ALEXEY
(*From outside*)
Misha! Are you coming?

MISHA
Goodbye, Dyedushka.

RABBI
Happy new year, my child, happy new year . . .

MISHA
I'll be back.

ALEXEY
(*From outside*)
Misha!

RABBI
I hope so, my child.

MISHA
I promise . . . You'll see.

RABBI
Go, my child. Go with your mother and father. They are waiting for you. Go with them. I hope they know where they're going. I don't. I don't even know where *I* am going. I even wonder whether your father isn't right—whether I am going anywhere at all.

MISHA

You'll see, Dyedushka, I will come back, I promise.
You'll see . . .

RABBI

Thank you, child, thank you for your promise. (MISHA
exits) Yes, I will see, I will see what I refused to see. I
will see what I no longer see.
(*Crumpled in his armchair, the* RABBI *stares into the
void. Now he knows he is alone and doomed. Nothing of
him will survive him. This is the moment* ZALMEN
chooses to push him to the wall)

ZALMEN

Well, Rabbi? Are you having doubts . . . regrets? You
seem depressed. Things aren't going too well, are they?
Why not follow my advice? Why not follow me?

RABBI
(*Weary*)
Zalmen, Zalmen . . . What do you want of me?

ZALMEN

I've told you. Let go, Rabbi, let yourself go mad!

RABBI

That's all?

ZALMEN

That's enough.

RABBI

And then? What happens then, Zalmen?

ZALMEN

Let the future take care of the future. Make this one evening count. This is a unique occasion and you know it. Your only chance. Don't let it slip away, Rabbi. If you do, you're a coward!

RABBI

A coward or simply a man trapped by habit? Is it our fault we have forgotten how to walk alone, how to take risks, how to venture forth on unknown paths? Can you condemn us for that? It's not courage we lack, but knowledge. Some elementary notions were erased from our minds. We no longer know how to do or undo certain things—we have forgotten how to shout, how to vent our anger, how to say no.

ZALMEN

You lack imagination, Rabbi! You've lost hope. That's bad enough, but worse—you've closed yourself to imagination! That's unforgivable, Rabbi! For we are the imagination and madness of the world—we are imagination gone mad. One has to be mad today to believe in God and in man—one has to be mad to believe. One has to be mad to want to remain human. Be mad, Rabbi, be mad!

RABBI

Zalmen, Zalmen, you are cruel . . .

ZALMEN

I have no choice. I owe it to myself, to you. Become mad tonight—just tonight—and God on His throne will envy you your light. You're afraid—I know. Don't be—

not tonight. Madness is an answer to fear. Become mad tonight and fear will shatter at your feet, harmless and wretched. Hear me, Rabbi—hold on to me and go beyond me! Do it, Rabbi, and we will laugh together. Will we laugh together . . .

RABBI

Not so easy, Zalmen, not so easy. Fear and I, we have shared the same roof for a long, long time.

ZALMEN

Tear your fear out by the root! Let it not become your night and your universe, your silence and your lie—or, what is worse, your truth, your God!

RABBI
(*Visibly at the end of his endurance*)
Zalmen . . .

ZALMEN

Become a rabbi once more. A shepherd. A leader who points the way. A keeper of the flame. A smasher of idols. One outcry, Rabbi—one word, one gesture—will open the gates of legend to you.

RABBI

I am old, too old for gestures of this sort. Too old to follow you, to understand you. If I were younger . . .

ZALMEN

You were young and you did nothing!

RABBI

That was a mistake. Too late to correct it now. More than you, I need a *rebbe*.

ZALMEN
(*Staring at the* RABBI)
And what if *I* were your *rebbe?*

RABBI
(*In panic*)
You? My *rebbe?* No, no. It's unthinkable. A *rebbe* is someone who teaches humility, forgiveness. Someone who brings wisdom and serenity.

ZALMEN
That was true long ago. What if today he were some-one who drives you to pain, to torture, to madness?

RABBI
(*In a daze*)
I don't want to think about it . . .

ZALMEN
(*Disillusioned*)
I understand you, but I feel sorry for you. You haven't fought, and yet, here you are, defeated. You have prayed for nothing—lived for nothing; it is as though you have not lived at all . . . Did you hear what I said? I am waiting.

RABBI

Waiting for what?

ZALMEN

I am waiting for you.

RABBI

No, no, Zalmen. No! What do you take me for? Find
yourself another rabbi for tonight. Let *him* pound the
pulpit. And in the presence of our brothers from abroad
let *him* shout—let *him* shriek—that the Jewish soul is in
peril here and that it is being choked. No, Zalmen,
no . . . (*He rises, and suddenly he seems taller, majestic. On the
pulpit, to the right of the Ark, a candle is lit.* ZALMEN *removes
a tallith from its bag and drapes it over the old man's shoulders*) Tonight, as last year and the year before, I shall
recite the ancient prayer of the oppressed, the per-
secuted, the prisoners of silence: *Kol Nidre, Veesorei, Veki-
nuyei, Vekonamei* . . . We proclaim ourselves free from
false promises, from vows taken under duress. What we
have said is now unsaid. We aspire to a moment of truth,
and if that truth shall bring us nothing but tears, so be it.
But our bonds shall not be bonds and only by our tears
shall we abide. (*There is a change of lighting. Sounds.*
ZALMEN *moves into the background. One gets the feeling of
being in the synagogue—one can hear the noise of the crowd*)
I say and I proclaim—I say and I proclaim—that it is more
than we can bear! You, our brothers who see us now,
hear the last cries of a shattered community! To you I say:
The sparks are dying and our heritage, our very destiny
are covered with dust. Broken are the wings of the eagle,
the lion is ill. And I say and I proclaim to any who will
listen that the Torah here is in peril and the spirit of a
whole people is being crushed. (*A hush falls over the hall.
One of the guards moves quickly to extinguish the candles. Some
of the congregants are seen backing away toward the exit; others*

merely lower their heads in shame) And all the sufferings
. . . the faith, the obstinate and desperate courage, the
allegiance to a covenant three thousand years old will
have been for nothing . . . for nothing. If we allow this
to continue, if you, our brothers, forsake us, we will be
the last of the Jews in this land, the last witnesses, the last
of the Jews who in silence bury the Jew within them. And
know this, brothers who leave without having spoken to
us, that so much silence is breaking my heart, that hope
has deserted me. Know that it is more than I can bear,
it is more than I can bear . . .

Act Two

The next day. Night.

The stage is unchanged, except for the lighting: bare, intense white beams. In the corner a small table has been added for the SECRETARY, *a woman of no particular age or personality. She takes notes without looking up, without showing any interest in what she is writing.*

Outside, the silhouette of a GUARD *in uniform. Off to one side, figures of witnesses. Anyone who has had contact with the* RABBI *during the twenty-four hours leading up to the incident has been summoned. Now that the visitors from abroad are gone, the investigation can begin.*

The INSPECTOR *will conduct the interrogation with a friendly but nervous voice. From time to time he will consult in whispers with the high-ranking* POLICE OFFICIAL *who, seated in the background, will only rarely intervene.*

The POLICE OFFICIAL, *bald, with a deeply lined face, impassive, distant, chain-smoking, seems bored.*

The RABBI *seems older. Having performed his sacrificial act, he looks spent. Glassy-eyed, seemingly detached, he listens to the questions, and answers in a tired, resigned voice.*

The mood is tense, oppressive.

INSPECTOR

Do you realize what you have done? In front of foreigners—important guests of our government! What will they think of us—of you?

RABBI

I don't know . . .

INSPECTOR

Dammit, what came over you all of a sudden? What happened? Who's behind this? Who provoked you—and why?

RABBI

I have told you everything. Everything I know.

INSPECTOR

(*Angry*)

What did you tell me? That it was an outburst of temper? An impulsive act? A momentary lapse? A whim?

RABBI

A moment . . . a moment of unconsciousness, of falling . . . upwards. A strange moment of dizziness. It came, it went. Then it was over.

INSPECTOR

For you perhaps. Not for us. We are just beginning.

RABBI

For me it is over. I told you: it was *not* premeditated. I have explained . . .

INSPECTOR

Your explanations are dismally inadequate, you know that.

RABBI

I am tired . . . And then, it all seems so far, so very far away.

INSPECTOR

Far? Yesterday? You've forgotten what happened yesterday?

RABBI

I haven't forgotten anything. But it is far, farther and farther away. I see someone and I don't recognize myself.

INSPECTOR

(*Exchanges a look with the* POLICE OFFICIAL)
Whom do you see?

RABBI

A man. Shrouded in fog. At the bottom of a mountain he is trying to scale. He is turning around, he's motioning to someone. To me perhaps. A sign of farewell. Or of reproach. He speaks to me—but I cannot hear what he is saying. He is too far away.

INSPECTOR

So—you're a visionary now! You see spirits, you hear voices! Are you making fun of us?

RABBI

No. Not of you.

INSPECTOR

Thank you—that's very generous of you. (*He pauses*)
Listen to me and listen carefully. Stop playing games.
Those hallucinations, keep them for your Jews. We are
here for a purpose: to investigate a serious matter—to
define responsibilities—to evaluate the implications and
follow every lead. Do you understand?

RABBI

I'm trying . . .

INSPECTOR

Try harder. Think of your community. You have
placed it in danger. Think!

RABBI

I am trying my best . . .

INSPECTOR

I hope so—for their sake. Let's start all over again.
From the beginning. Tell us what happened. I mean—
what really happened.

RABBI

Then something really did happen?

INSPECTOR

Rabbi, please!

RABBI

I beg your pardon. I don't mean to deny anything . . .

90

INSPECTOR

Thank God for that!

RABBI

But still, I wonder if . . . if what happened was—how shall I say—real . . . yes, real. It is the reality of the event that escapes me, not the event itself. Is that so hard to understand?

INSPECTOR

Frankly, Rabbi, yes, it is.

RABBI

Yet I am trying, but I'm not finding the words. All this seems to me so . . . so . . . I was going to say so confused. But that's not it. Confusion is not the exact term—the images are clear enough. Indeed, they're luminous. Blinding.

INSPECTOR

Congratulations. At last you are emerging from the fog.

RABBI

Yes, everything is clear, precise, but . . .

INSPECTOR

But what?

RABBI

But impossible. It all seems so . . . impossible.

INSPECTOR

Why impossible?

RABBI

Perhaps because I thought I knew myself—who I am, what I want to achieve and what I must remember.

INSPECTOR

In other words, that man in the fog was not you?

RABBI

I wonder . . .

INSPECTOR

Enough! There is only one thing I want to know. What happened to you last night? What devil pushed you?

RABBI

I had a dream, that's all. And in my dream I came upon a dreamer—it was me.

INSPECTOR

So now I have *two* dreamers on my hands. One wasn't enough!

RABBI

Your generation is opposed to dreams—mine needs them. Every Jewish child is full of dreams—not always his own. He receives them and passes them on, and they are always the same: an ancient kingdom restored, peace on earth, the messianic victory of man over what makes him inhuman. Exciting, passionate dreams . . . They sound like prayers.

INSPECTOR

No prayers, please! (*He brutally changes tone*) Facts, stick to facts!

RABBI

I don't like facts. I don't even like dreams—I am afraid of the awakening. I prefer to remain on the other side.

INSPECTOR

The other side? But that's called madness!

RABBI

I don't like to name things.

INSPECTOR

You certainly don't like anything tonight. (*He is getting angrier by the minute*) Are you going to talk? I mean really talk? Yes or no?

RABBI

What I would be able to tell you, you already know. What you don't know, I could not tell you; it cannot be told.

INSPECTOR

Force yourself, Rabbi. After all, speech was given to man for a purpose.

RABBI

So was silence, Comrade Inspector. So was silence.

INSPECTOR

Too late, Rabbi. Yesterday was when you should have chosen silence.

RABBI

Yesterday I chose to speak, to share my dream—but now the dream is over. The rest is of no importance. I wish I could have passed on a word, a prayer, a tale, a fragment of a tale to whoever might need it. Perhaps to a child yet unborn. I have spoiled everything. Too late to start again. That child of mine will never be born.

INSPECTOR
(*Mocking*)

You're forgetting your God, Rabbi—let Him dream your dream!

RABBI

I have not forgotten Him, Comrade Inspector—I have never forgotten Him.

INSPECTOR

Could it be that . . . He has forgotten you? (*The* RABBI *is bewildered, grief-stricken. He would like to protest, to cast away his doubts but the cry does not leave his parted lips. The* INSPECTOR *consults with the* POLICE OFFICIAL *for a moment before turning back to the* RABBI) Just the facts. (*He lowers his voice, seething*) Why did you do it? Why?

RABBI

I don't know . . . I no longer know. I no longer know what I was thinking—what it was I knew then. I only know that it's too late to turn back. Too late to invent a meaning for something that perhaps had none—too late for apologies.

INSPECTOR

How could you—a wise and respectable man—how could you have thought up such nonsense? You who have lived through so much—you must have been aware of the risks! Overt incitement against the government . . . Libelous lies to please and strengthen our enemies . . . What was your motive? Your goal? Whom were you serving? What did you wish to obtain or prove?

RABBI

You won't understand. It's too late . . . even to understand.

INSPECTOR

Try! Try to explain! Don't tell me it's too late to try? (*He pauses, and continues in a conciliatory tone*) I would like to help you, but I must understand. Trust me, and I'll do whatever I can.

RABBI

What do you want me to do? Declare myself guilty? Beg for mercy? Confess my sins? Is that what you want? I am ready to do it. I hereby declare that I am guilty. Guilty of all the offenses. You are free to enlarge the list —add anything you wish. I will sign everything. Are you satisfied?

INSPECTOR

Names. We want names . . . all the names.

RABBI

My name is . . .

INSPECTOR

Not yours!

RABBI

Mine is the only one I know—and even that, not always.

INSPECTOR

Are you starting that again?

RABBI

No . . . no. I am not starting again. I promise you.

INSPECTOR

For the last time I ask you to tell us the truth—the whole truth!

RABBI

I can't. My strength is gone. Sentences tear apart inside me. Words are drained of meaning, they fly away, disperse and fall on me like enemies. They strangle me.

INSPECTOR
(*Dumbfounded*)

Who's strangling you?

RABBI

The words. Those I speak and those I omit. And all the others, those I have warped, mutilated, debased—now they take vengeance.

INSPECTOR
(*To the* POLICE OFFICIAL)
He's raving . . . This is sheer madness!

RABBI
(*Delirious*)
Sheer madness, pure and impure madness, dark madness, liberating madness, salutory madness . . . Let it come—I won't resist any more. I'll welcome it with open arms. May it lend me its voice . . . its darkness . . . its force.

INSPECTOR
(*Playing along*)
And the sermon . . . madness too?

RABBI
Pure madness. *Kol Nidre?* Madness. The sermon . . . what sermon? I didn't hear any sermons. All I heard was madness—and soon it will all be over. No more questions, no more answers, no more sermons, no more threats, no more remorse—no more anything.

INSPECTOR
(*Looks at him with feigned admiration*)
Well now—at last we are being offered an explanation. And it's magnificent! But madness doesn't strike all of a sudden, just like that, without warning, like a wild beast pouncing on its prey! Madness has a history, a beginning —it smolders inside you, it burns, then it overflows and explodes. But tell us: What caused the explosion?

RABBI

It will take too long to tell. And it's too late for words. Also, I am tired—extremely tired. I would like to close my eyes and quietly withdraw from life.

INSPECTOR

Wait a moment! First—answer! When did you start plotting? When was the first time? The first impulse? The first decision, the first secret . . . when?

RABBI

(*Eyes closed*)

I don't know when. I don't know anything. I can see your questions; they are dark, cruel birds. Do I wish to follow them or destroy them? I don't know. I don't know who you are. Or who I am.

INSPECTOR

(*Offers him a glass of water*)

You're tired, Rabbi. It's only natural. Yesterday's excitement. The long fast. (*The* RABBI *drinks*) There—that's better. Stop resisting us, and you'll get your rest. You need it and you'll have earned it. Now then . . . When . . .

RABBI

(*In a fit of anger*)

You have just that one question on your tongue! When, when, when! How do I know when? And what difference does it make? Today, yesterday, last week, last year—a century ago . . .

98

INSPECTOR

But why now? Why this of all times? Was it the presence of the foreigners? Or was there something else?

RABBI

(*Sinks back in the chair*)

I am old. Do what you will with me. I won't protest. Send me to prison, to exile or to death. I am ready.

INSPECTOR

(*Stares at him*)

What about the others? Who hired you? A member of the synagogue? A stranger? An angel from heaven perhaps?

RABBI

(*Weary, almost detached*)

So you refuse to understand. I am alone—do you hear? I am alone, and my secret is my own. I shared it with no one!

INSPECTOR

No one?

RABBI

No one! It is my secret and mine alone! Leave the others out of this, they are innocent. I swear it—I alone am responsible, I alone am guilty, do you hear? I am guilty and demand to be punished—and I will accept my punishment in silence, yes, in *silence!*

(*Exhausted, his eyes half closed, the* RABBI *from now on will be silent. He has played and lost. Since his world has gone bankrupt, he will remain locked in his silence. Is he*

listening? Is he even present? He is with ZALMEN. *He is*
ZALMEN)

INSPECTOR

Is this some new tactic? (*The* RABBI *does not answer*)
And you hope it will serve a purpose? (*The* RABBI *still
does not answer*) Don't you see? It is too late for silence!
(*There is no reaction from the* RABBI)

POLICE OFFICIAL
(*Sarcastic*)

Do we go on?

INSPECTOR
(*After some hesitation*)

Call in the Chairman. (*Again he pauses*) Rabbi, you
stay. I believe in confrontations.
(*The* CHAIRMAN *is obviously nervous though he enters
with a firm step, greets the officials but avoids looking at
the* RABBI, *who seems not to see him either*)

INSPECTOR

I am glad you were able to come. Be seated, please.
(*The* CHAIRMAN *hesitates and takes a seat to the left of the*
RABBI, *still without looking at him*) My colleague and I are
very sorry to have disturbed you at so late an hour. But
in view of your official position . . .

CHAIRMAN
(*Aggressive*)

No apologies are necessary. I asked to be present at
this interrogation.

INSPECTOR
(*Conciliatory*)

That is correct. Anyway, you are not personally implicated in this affair. Anyone else perhaps—but not you.

CHAIRMAN

And why not me?

INSPECTOR
(*Taken aback*)

I beg your pardon . . .

CHAIRMAN

Why not me?

INSPECTOR

I know you. You're a realist, not a hothead. And no fool.

CHAIRMAN

I appreciate your compliments.

INSPECTOR

Am I wrong?

CHAIRMAN

You were saying that I am not implicated . . . meaning that others are. But who?

INSPECTOR

That's what we are here to find out. I am counting on you to make our task easier.

CHAIRMAN

In this unfortunate affair, we—the leaders and members of our synagogue—have played no part. For us, as for you, the incident in question was as distressing as it was unexpected.

INSPECTOR

Then, in your opinion . . .

CHAIRMAN

This is not my opinion—I know.

INSPECTOR

How can you be so sure?

CHAIRMAN
(*Interrupts*)

Like you, I am a good judge of men. I know my people. They can hide nothing from me. I know their problems, I interpret their anguish. I know the boundaries of their courage. Satisfied or not, none will ever get involved in a scandal such as this. Ever!

INSPECTOR

Why not?

CHAIRMAN
(*Stiffens*)

Because they are afraid. It's as simple as that. Afraid. Fear is the safest of boundaries.

INSPECTOR
(*Offended*)
Under our Socialist justice the innocent have nothing
to fear.

CHAIRMAN
You know that and I know that. Most of my people
do not.

INSPECTOR
Still, how can you possibly vouch for every one of
them?

CHAIRMAN
I can and I do. If any others are guilty, then I am too.
Guilty of incompetence. Guilty of having been blind.
(*The* INSPECTOR *makes a gesture of protest. The* CHAIRMAN
goes on) But no one is guilty. That sermon—we never
discussed it, not even afterwards. We simply ignored it.

INSPECTOR
But, Comrade Chairman . . .

CHAIRMAN
Fear corrects memory and my people are afraid! Yes.
Must I remind you that some of them still keep a carefully
packed suitcase close to their beds . . . just in case?

INSPECTOR
Yet *you* don't give the impression of being afraid?

CHAIRMAN

My situation is different—you need me. You know
that as well as I do.

INSPECTOR

My dear Chairman, do understand . . . It is our duty
to consider all possibilities, all hypotheses. How can you
be sure that certain dissatisfied individuals did not play
a role in all this?

CHAIRMAN

Do you by any chance imagine that I am content?
Always? That I approve of all your measures? That I
applaud them? I don't—and I have never concealed this
from you. But does that mean that I would participate—
even indirectly—in such a spectacle?

INSPECTOR
(*Slyly*)

As a matter of fact—why not? What would be holding
you back?

CHAIRMAN

My sense of responsibility to the community. It needs
a leader, not a martyr.

INSPECTOR

And what if the community felt that, quite the contrary, what it needed . . . was a martyr?

CHAIRMAN

It doesn't—no Jewish community ever does! We have
had too many. The history of our people is swimming in

the blood and tears of its children. Today, Jews need realists, not saints glorifying sacrifice. We have only one mission: to survive. To survive at any cost!

INSPECTOR

In that case you cannot condemn the Rabbi for having done in his way what you are trying to accomplish in yours: to help Jews survive. He may be of the opinion that they greatly need a martyr . . . (*He pauses*) Suppose the Rabbi acted according to his conscience and for the good of your community—would you blame him? Yes or no? (*In the face of the* CHAIRMAN's *silence, he raises his voice*) Yes or no?

CHAIRMAN
(*Hostile but composed*)

I came here—voluntarily—to speak to you about the Synagogue Council of which I am the head. Not about the Rabbi.

INSPECTOR
(*Ironic*)

Does his presence embarrass you? We can ask him to wait outside.

CHAIRMAN

No! It is one of my principles to tell people what I think of them in their presence.

INSPECTOR

Well? Tell him.

CHAIRMAN
(*Losing his temper*)
What would you like to hear me say? That I condemn
him? I won't.

INSPECTOR
Then . . . you are defending him.

CHAIRMAN
I didn't say that. I said that I would not condemn a
lonely man who has just set the whole world against him.
His sermon may mean trouble for us—that's what people
are saying, the very people for whom he was so eager to
sacrifice himself. They don't want his sacrifice. And you
want me to reject him? I shall not condemn him, do you
hear me? Never!

INSPECTOR
I think you envy him.

CHAIRMAN
For what? His heroism? I prefer the everyday kind of
courage. For his solitude perhaps? (*He hesitates before con-
tinuing*) Do you suppose that I am not alone? That people
love me and show me their affection? That they smile as
they wish me a happy new year? That they invite me to
their celebrations, and share my mourning? For them—
I represent the other side: yours!

INSPECTOR
Well now, here *you* are—our newest martyr!

CHAIRMAN

Spare me your irony. My solitude is my business.

INSPECTOR

And the Rabbi's solitude?

CHAIRMAN

The Rabbi's solitude is my business as well. And I find his solitude heavy to bear—heavier than mine—because his anguish is greater than mine. Spiritual things matter more to him than to me. I am the last of my family, but he is the last of a tradition; he is the last Rabbi of this community. He knows it. So do I, but I made my peace with it. If God wishes this town to be without Jews, so be it. But can you imagine what this means to him? (*He points to the* RABBI) Do you know what it means to be the last teacher, the last messenger, the last believer? What it means to realize that one's truth will be lost and one's ideals forgotten? Do you know what it means to witness silently, day after day, week after week, the disappearance—worse, the distortion—of one's faith, one's image, one's past in front of one's very eyes? That's all I have to say.

INSPECTOR

(*Mocking but friendly*)

You see? We tolerate critics—I'd even say we encourage them. (*He pauses*) However, don't go following the Rabbi's example!

CHAIRMAN

(*Gets up*)

Do you need me any further?

INSPECTOR
Aren't you interested in what comes next?

CHAIRMAN
I'm interested in only one thing: what you are going
to do with the Rabbi.

INSPECTOR
Does that really concern you that much?

CHAIRMAN
That much.

INSPECTOR
In spite of everything?

CHAIRMAN
Because of everything.

POLICE OFFICIAL
Aha . . . another hero!

CHAIRMAN
(*With dignity*)
In my capacity of Chairman of this community, I have
the right to ask you what you intend to do with the
Rabbi.

INSPECTOR
(*Conciliatory*)
That all depends on what develops.

CHAIRMAN
In that case may I stay?

INSPECTOR
(*Consults the* POLICE OFFICIAL; *consents*)
Next witness! Malkin!
(*The* INSPECTOR *casts a glance at his papers. The*
GUARD *shouts the* DOCTOR*'s name several times. There
are various sounds of goings and comings*)

GUARD
(*At attention*)
The witness isn't here, Comrade Inspector.

INSPECTOR
(*Surprised, irritated*)
Hasn't he been summoned?

GUARD
He has.

INSPECTOR
Call the hospital. If the witness is there, have him sent
to me at once.

GUARD
At once, Comrade Inspector.
(*The* GUARD *exits*)

INSPECTOR
Did he notify our office that he'd be late?

SECRETARY

No, Comrade Inspector.

CHAIRMAN

Don't worry about him. He'll have a good excuse, like having been detained at the hospital, for example.
(*The* GUARD *reappears*)

GUARD

The witness is not at the hospital.

INSPECTOR

Try his home.

GUARD

We already did, Comrade Inspector. We talked to his wife. He hasn't been home all day—she says.

INSPECTOR

Strange. Very strange.

POLICE OFFICIAL

You mean suspicious.

INSPECTOR
(*Irritated. To the* GUARD)
I want you to find him. Check his friends, his neighbors, his patients. At once.

GUARD

Yes, Comrade Inspector.
(*The* GUARD *starts to leave*)

POLICE OFFICIAL

Wait. (*He scribbles a few words on a piece of paper*) Call this number. They'll know what to do.

(*The* GUARD *leaves to execute the orders. The* INSPECTOR *goes into the waiting room, as though to convince himself of the* DOCTOR*'s absence. While the* INSPECTOR *talks to witnesses outside, the* POLICE OFFICIAL *lights a cigarette and offers one to the* CHAIRMAN. *Both listen to the voices coming from the other room*)

INSPECTOR
(*To the unseen Councillors*)

Where is Dr. Malkin? (*There is a faint chorus of responses:* Don't know . . . No idea . . . How could we . . .) Why isn't he here yet? (*Chorus:* No idea . . . Inconceivable . . . Can't understand . . .) Didn't anyone know he would be delayed? (*Chorus:* No . . . no idea . . . I wasn't . . . he wasn't . . . No, impossible . . .) All right—we'll see— we'll get to the bottom of this mess! Come in! All of you! Let's go! (*The Councillors appear. They look frozen with terror*) Well? (*The* INSPECTOR *goes from one to the other, scanning their faces*) One member of your Council is missing. I want to know why. If he has disappeared, I want to know when—and with whom. I want to know where he is. And you are going to tell me. (*To* CHAIM) When did you see him last?

CHAIM

Today. This morning. Like everybody else. At services.

ZENDER

Me too. At services. Like everybody else.

INSPECTOR

Who saw him in the afternoon?

MOTKE

(*Faced with the* INSPECTOR*'s insistent look*)
Me? I saw him leave . . . he was called by a patient . . .

INSPECTOR

What time was that?

MOTKE

After the *Mussaf* prayer. About four o'clock . . . or five . . .

INSPECTOR

And he never came back? And no one knows where he went? (*There is a general silence*) Never mind. We'll find him. Let's talk about you—all of you. Let's talk about yesterday. Does anyone want to make a statement? (*The Councillors remain silent*) So. Nobody's going to open his mouth. The most talkative people on earth—struck dumb? The best-informed tribe in the world suddenly knows nothing? (*To* CHAIM) You didn't know what was going to happen last night—right? (*To* MOTKE) And you had no inkling of anything—did you? (*To* SHMUEL) You didn't see or hear a thing? (*To everybody*) You spent that whole morning with the Rabbi and yet you knew nothing of his plans—nothing—and you expect me to believe that?

CHAIRMAN
(*Emphatically*)
I protest against these insinuations!

INSPECTOR
You keep out of this!

CHAIRMAN
As Chairman of this community I have the right and
the duty to speak up. My colleagues here have nothing
to do with all this!

INSPECTOR
I question whomever I please, in the way I please!

CHAIRMAN
You're treating them like suspects—and in that case,
you must include me too! Furthermore, I herewith sub-
mit my resignation effective as of this moment! Find
yourself another Chairman!
(*The two men take each other's measure. The* INSPEC-
TOR *chooses to yield*)

INSPECTOR
Why get all upset? None of your colleagues has been
accused of anything.

CHAIRMAN
I'm glad to hear you say it.
(The CHAIRMAN *sits down again. A silence follows,
broken by* CHAIM *trying to chase away the uneasiness*)

INSPECTOR
This investigation is being held here, not at the Ministry . . .

CHAIM
For us, it was a terrible misfortune.

SRUL
Yes, what a misfortune!

SHMUEL
We expected everything but that.

ZENDER
Who could have foreseen . . .

GUARD
(*Reports to the* INSPECTOR)
Still no news.
(*The* GUARD *whispers to the* POLICE OFFICIAL, *then
returns to his post. Meanwhile the action continues*)

CHAIRMAN
I can't see what difference it will make—whether he
shows up or not. He doesn't know any more than we do.

INSPECTOR
I wonder . . . (*He gets an idea*) Which of you spoke with
the Rabbi alone yesterday?

CHAIM
Not me.

SHMUEL

No, certainly not me.

ZENDER

We never speak alone.

MOTKE

We left immediately after the meeting.

CHAIM

Right away.

SRUL

Together . . . at the same time.

INSPECTOR

At the same time? All of you?

CHAIRMAN

The Doctor and I stayed on for a moment.

INSPECTOR

Oh?

CHAIRMAN

We had one of our "friendly" little discussions.

INSPECTOR

Right here?

CHAIRMAN

Right here.

INSPECTOR

And then?

CHAIRMAN

We left.

INSPECTOR

You went . . . home?

CHAIRMAN

Where else would I go?

INSPECTOR

And he? He stayed behind?

CHAIRMAN

I suppose so.

INSPECTOR

Here?

CHAIRMAN

Yes—here.

INSPECTOR

Alone?

CHAIRMAN
(*Hesitates*)

Yes.

INSPECTOR

Not entirely alone. With the Rabbi.

116

CHAIRMAN
What are you driving at?

INSPECTOR
First, the Rabbi and the Doctor meet in the morning
—alone. Second, some hours later the Rabbi explodes his
bomb. Third, though duly summoned, the Doctor has
decided not to appear. I simply wonder whether these
three facts—I repeat: facts—are not related.

CHAIRMAN
You suspect *him?*

INSPECTOR
Why not? After all, why couldn't he, too, have wanted
to contribute in his way to what you call the spiritual
survival of your people?

CHAIRMAN
(*Harshly*)
Listen to me—I don't like the man and I have certainly
no desire to defend him. But don't try to make him into
a hero or a martyr!

INSPECTOR
A man of your experience should not take anything
about anybody for granted.

CHAIRMAN
Only a man of my experience can take that risk.

INSPECTOR
Last week, would you have vouched for . . . the Rabbi?

CHAIRMAN

Without the slightest hesitation. And I would have
been wrong.

INSPECTOR

Well?

CHAIRMAN

Well, nothing! You cannot compare the two. The
Rabbi is a Jew through and through. When he weeps, it
is the Jew in him grieving. When he keeps silent, it is the
Jew in him despairing of language. As for the other one,
he doesn't cry, he doesn't weep, he doesn't despair. For
him, to be a Jew is an option, a concept—devoid of
mystery. And concepts, as you know, can change, adjust,
or even vanish. Anyway, they don't hurt. No, these two
men have nothing in common.

INSPECTOR

I admire your confidence in your own judgment. Still,
what if you were wrong? Eh? Just this once?

CHAIRMAN
(*Looks for an argument; finds it*)
The Rabbi is here; let's ask him if I'm wrong. (*Gently,
to the* RABBI) I beg of you, Rabbi, speak. This is important. (*The* RABBI *looks at him but remains silent*) Please
. . . help us. Don't permit your silence to be misinter-
preted . . . I beg of you.

RABBI
(*Weakly*)
I . . . alone . . . am guilty. I alone . . .

INSPECTOR

He's in another world.

CHAIRMAN

But he answered! You heard him!

INSPECTOR

I'd rather hear what the Doctor has to say. Next witness!

SECRETARY

Adamov!
(ALEXEY *enters, followed by* NINA *and* MISHA. NINA *is biting her lips.* MISHA *doesn't take his eyes off his grandfather.* ALEXEY, *to cover his embarrassment, speaks with somewhat exaggerated authority*)

ALEXEY

Adamov, Alexey, engineer, Comrades. My wife . . .

INSPECTOR
(*Continues*)

Nina and your son Misha. Good evening. You should have left him home.

ALEXEY

Misha doesn't like to be treated like a child, not even by his parents.

NINA

He insisted on coming . . .

INSPECTOR

He did?

ALEXEY

He's a big boy, don't worry about him.

INSPECTOR

How old are you, Misha?
(MISHA, *staring at the* RABBI, *does not hear the question*)

ALEXEY

Misha! How old are you?

MISHA
(*Tense*)

Twelve.

INSPECTOR

Almost a man . . .

NINA

Still a child.

INSPECTOR

Children grow up fast these days. (*To* ALEXEY *and* NINA) Does he know?

ALEXEY

Only that something has happened; he doesn't know what.

INSPECTOR

It's late, Misha. Aren't you sleepy?

MISHA

No.

INSPECTOR

It's past bedtime . . .

MISHA

No.

ALEXEY

Sometimes he's as stubborn as . . . (*He looks at the* RABBI) as his mother.

NINA

He's a good boy.

INSPECTOR

You should go home, Misha. Tomorrow, in class, you won't be able to open your eyes.

MISHA

I will.

INSPECTOR

Why are you so anxious to be here tonight?

NINA

He's just a child . . .

INSPECTOR

What are you afraid of? To remain at home alone?

MISHA

I'm not afraid.

INSPECTOR

Of course not. So there must be another reason . . .

MISHA

My grandfather.

INSPECTOR

Yes?

MISHA

I wanted to see him.

INSPECTOR

But you saw him, didn't you? Only yesterday?

MISHA

I wanted to see him again.

NINA

Misha doesn't see him often.

INSPECTOR

Oh? Why not?

ALEXEY
(*Quickly*)

He's busy with school.

INSPECTOR
(*To* MISHA)
So you love him that much?

MISHA
He's my grandfather and I love him very much.

INSPECTOR
(*To* ALEXEY *and* NINA)
You'll be proud of him; he has character. By the way,
where were you last night?

ALEXEY
Not at the synagogue.

NINA
Home. We stayed home. Some friends came over to
visit.

ALEXEY
Gubanov and his wife. Works with me at the factory.

INSPECTOR
Did they stay late?

ALEXEY
Fairly late.

INSPECTOR
Then—who told you?

ALEXEY
We heard rumors.

INSPECTOR

When?

ALEXEY

This morning.

INSPECTOR

But there was nothing in the newspapers . . .

ALEXEY

News travels fast here, Comrade. Especially bad news.
Our neighbors are always the first to know everything.

INSPECTOR
(*To* NINA)

And what exactly were those rumors?

NINA

Nothing much. Nothing definite. Just that my father
. . . that the Rabbi had made a terrible speech, eh, sermon.

INSPECTOR

Why terrible?

NINA

The people didn't know . . . didn't know what he said.

INSPECTOR

But you guessed?

NINA

No . . . (*After some hesitation*) No.

INSPECTOR

And what was your reaction?

NINA

I refused to believe it.

INSPECTOR

Why?

NINA

Because . . . because . . .

ALEXEY
(*Helping her out*)
Because we are not used to paying attention to rumors.

INSPECTOR

So when those rumors reached you, what did you do?

ALEXEY

Nothing.

INSPECTOR
(*Looks at* ALEXEY, *then turns his attention back to* NINA)
You didn't run to the synagogue? To see? To find out?

NINA

My first impulse was . . . to run here. To see if . . .

INSPECTOR

If what?

NINA

If he was still here.

INSPECTOR
(*Ironic*)
So you came here?

ALEXEY
Nobody went anywhere.

INSPECTOR
Weren't you worried?

ALEXEY
I have faith in our justice. We don't harm pitiful old
men who talk too much.

INSPECTOR
(*To* NINA)
But you . . .

NINA
He's my father . . . after all. He's old. Sick. Unhappy.
I . . . I never did bring him any joy. Only pain. Much
pain.

INSPECTOR
I see. (*He watches* MISHA, *who has been staring at the*
RABBI, *spellbound*) What about you, my young comrade,
what do you think your grandfather did last night?

MISHA
Something very serious . . . something no one ever did
before.

126

(*The* RABBI *moves imperceptibly. He sighs. His eyes wander over to the boy. A brief smile lights up his face*)

NINA
(*Gets hold of herself*)
My father would never cause a scandal. He's a gentle human being. Sad. Peaceful. Withdrawn. Incapable of raising his voice—even in his own home. When I was little my mother would sometimes scold me, punish me. Not he. Never. But when I'd see that he was sad, I knew that I had done something wrong.

INSPECTOR
The father you remember and the Rabbi . . . are they the same person?

NINA
My father hasn't changed. All of us have changed—he has not.

ALEXEY
She's right. As long as I've known him he's been the same. You can't get him angry. It's useless to try. Even my anger never had any effect on him.

INSPECTOR
Comrade Adamov, you visited here yesterday—didn't you?

ALEXEY
Not exactly. It could hardly be called a visit.

INSPECTOR

You quarreled?

NINA

No.

ALEXEY

Yes.

INSPECTOR

Yes or no?

ALEXEY

Yes and no. I lost my temper. Once more. Tolerance is not my greatest virtue. I told him things I had told him a thousand times before—that if he wanted to pray, that was fine with me. But to stop trying to convert us, to stop meddling in our lives. And—above all—to leave my son alone.

POLICE OFFICIAL

How did he take all that?

ALEXEY

Calmly. As usual.

NINA

He was sad. Sadder than usual.

INSPECTOR

And you had no inkling of what he was to do that very night?

NINA

He was sad when he wished us a happy new year. As
sad as on the day I told him that I was going to marry
Alexey.

POLICE OFFICIAL

Please stick to the point. (*To* ALEXEY) What did you
think of his speech?

ALEXEY

Senseless. Like his lamentations, his prayers.

POLICE OFFICIAL

Had you known he was preparing such a speech, what
would you have done?

ALEXEY

I would have done my best to dissuade him.

INSPECTOR

And what if he had remained stubborn?

ALEXEY

I would have kept on trying.

POLICE OFFICIAL

Until . . . ?

ALEXEY
(*After a silence*)

I would have done my duty.

INSPECTOR

You mean . . . you would have told us? Why? Since all this was of no importance . . .

ALEXEY

Still, I would have done my duty. Only . . .

INSPECTOR

Yes?

ALEXEY

I would have added that this silly old man deserves pity rather than punishment.

POLICE OFFICIAL

But you must admit that from an objective and legal point of view his speech constitutes a serious violation of the law. You don't mean to suggest that silly old people are above the law . . . do you?

(*All eyes are on* ALEXEY. *He must take a stand*)

ALEXEY

(*Weighing every word*)

I have always done my duty as a citizen and as a member of the Communist Party. Right now my duty compels me to point out your mistake. This old man managed to deceive all of you. His attack was directed not against the State, not against the regime, but against his son-in-law. Me. Yes, me. To embarrass me. To shame me. He resents me because I refuse to follow in the footsteps of my so-called ancestors. But most of all, he hates me because, when I married his only daughter, I didn't at the same time marry the faith of her childhood, and because, renegade that I am, I robbed him of his last hope—his only grandson. So he caused a scandal to demonstrate to me the power of his weapons, since he could not convince me of the merits of his conviction that whether I want it or not, in the eyes of others, I am considered a Jew and always will be—and that whether I like it or not, my lot remains tied to that of all Jews of all times—everywhere. He wanted to show me that were I to be even indirectly implicated, my position would become insecure. You see, by giving him too much importance, you're playing his game. You must take this for what it is—a ridiculously annoying family quarrel.

INSPECTOR
(*Bewildered*)
Now, look here! You want to save your father-in-law, fine. But you can't be serious—is *that* really your interpretation?

ALEXEY
It's as plausible as any other! What? This old man—a dangerous enemy of the mighty Soviet Socialist State? A counterrevolutionary? Why would he have waited so long? He—and all of us—lived through infinitely more critical situations—remember? Why didn't he protest then?

INSPECTOR
All right. But it works both ways. If your father-in-law was meaning to harm you and you alone—why did he wait until now?

ALEXEY
Because we had the argument yesterday.

INSPECTOR
Your first . . . ?

ALEXEY
Our last. He realized that we would never be reconciled. And so he seized the first opportunity to hit back. Psychologically, I think that makes sense.

POLICE OFFICIAL
We would thank you, Comrade, not to mix psychology with politics, particularly when speaking of a Rabbi who seems thoroughly involved with theology.

ALEXEY
But that's your mistake, Comrade. This has nothing to do with politics!

INSPECTOR
Everything has to do with politics, Comrade. (*To* NINA) And you? What have you to add?

NINA
(*Does not grasp her husband's intention to save the* RABBI)
Oh, I don't know what to think. My father . . . Alexey . . . they're so different. My father objected to our marriage. I pleaded with him, telling him that I loved Alexey. He would answer me: How can you love a Jew who in moments of danger turns his back on his people? He accepted him, later, only because . . . of Misha.

INSPECTOR
How do *you* explain what happened?

NINA
(*On the verge of tears*)
I just don't know . . . I don't understand. Father and
I have drifted apart . . . Misha is our only link.

INSPECTOR
I have a question to ask you. No, I mean you. (*To*
ALEXEY) The Rabbi's speech is a clear-cut provocation.
Would you be prepared to denounce it?

ALEXEY
(*In a raucous voice*)
If you insist. But I would hope not to be obliged to act
in a manner contrary to my conviction that the sermon
was not meant as a provocation.

INSPECTOR
Of course. But would you denounce it?

ALEXEY
I have never shirked my duty, Comrade.

INSPECTOR
(*Smiles*)
I never doubted it, Comrade Adamov. (*He pauses*)
You do hate him, don't you?

ALEXEY
No.

Oh? I thought . . .

ALEXEY

I feel sorry for him, that's all. He's a poor old man
whose world is crumbling. His daughter has abandoned
him, his son-in-law rejects him, his grandson will not be
like him. He's the last of a long line. He is a poor old man
who in a flash of lucidity has opened his eyes only to
discover himself on the fringes of life and history; he can
see nothing but his past in ruins. Ashes everywhere. A
society that has no place for him. Too late to start all over
again. How can one hate such a man? He hates himself
enough. All I feel for him is pity.

INSPECTOR

Misha . . . (*The boy, aware of the importance of the moment,
is staring intently at his father. Both father and son seem deeply
troubled. For* MISHA, *too, the choice is harrowing. And yet the*
INSPECTOR *would like to spare the boy the sight of his grandfather—humiliated*) Misha! Do you hear me?

MISHA

I hear you.

ALEXEY

Leave my son out of this! He has nothing to do with
it!

INSPECTOR

Don't get upset, Comrade Adamov. Anyway, Misha's
free to go home and go to sleep. I suggested that to him,
didn't I?

MISHA

I'd rather stay.

INSPECTOR

Don't be stubborn . . . this once.

MISHA

I'd rather stay. It's the first time . . . (*He takes a step toward the* RABBI) The first time . . . that I see him like this.

INSPECTOR

Do you feel sorry for him?

MISHA

No, I don't think so.

INSPECTOR

Your father does.

MISHA

I don't. It's something else I feel. I don't know what I feel right now . . . I only know I . . . love him very much.

INSPECTOR

More than before?

MISHA

In a different way.

NINA

Misha doesn't know what he's saying—he is too young to understand.

INSPECTOR

Go home, Misha.

NINA

Thank you, thank you so much. Misha, did you hear?
You can go home now. It's late. Go and get some rest.

MISHA

And you?

NINA
(*To the* INSPECTOR)

May I . . .

INSPECTOR

Yes. You are free to go too.

NINA

And . . . my husband?

INSPECTOR
(*To* ALEXEY)

Take them home.

ALEXEY
(*To* NINA)

You go with Misha. I'll stay awhile.
(MISHA *and his mother move slowly toward the exit.*
ALEXEY *accompanies them*)

NINA

You don't think . . .

136

ALEXEY

Don't argue. Not now.

NINA

(*Takes* MISHA*'s arm*)

Come.

MISHA

(*Gently shakes himself loose*)

I want to stay.

(*Briefly the* RABBI*'s dark eyes come alive. Without saying
a word,* ALEXEY *sits down at the table, followed by* NINA
and MISHA. *The* INSPECTOR *and the* POLICE OFFI-
CIAL *exchange whispers. The* CHAIRMAN *clears his
throat*)

INSPECTOR

Next! Zalmen the Beadle!

GUARD

(*Appears, agitated*)

I beg your pardon, but . . .

INSPECTOR

(*Annoyed*)

The beadle!

GUARD

But . . .

INSPECTOR

What? Another one missing? I just saw him! He's preparing tea! Don't tell me he flew away?

137

GUARD

No, he's here. But we have two citizens who've seen the Doctor.

INSPECTOR
(*Jumps up*)

What?

GUARD

Two patients of his.

INSPECTOR
(*Shouts*)

What are you waiting for, dammit? Bring them in!
(*The* GUARD *opens the door and lets in* AVROM *and* FEIGE, *clinging one to the other. He is near fifty. She seems younger.* AVROM *is clutching a cap in his hand.* FEIGE *keeps mopping her face with a crumpled handkerchief. They remain standing*)

INSPECTOR

Names?

AVROM

Meirov, Avrom Davidovitch. Accountant. At the brush factory.

FEIGE

Feige. I'm his wife. Dressmaker . . .
(*Only now do they become aware of the* RABBI *and the Councillors. They speak quickly and together in chopped, almost incoherent sentences*)

AVROM

We were there . . .

FEIGE

. . . by accident.

AVROM

Strictly by accident.

FEIGE

We don't go to synagogues. We went . . .

AVROM

Out of curiosity.

FEIGE

But we didn't hear a thing.

AVROM

We left before . . .

FEIGE

. . . before we could hear a thing.

AVROM

Before *Kol Nidre* . . .

FEIGE

. . . before everyone else.

AVROM

We don't know a thing.

FEIGE
Yes—we left before everything . . .

AVROM
Before everything.

INSPECTOR
All right, we're not interested in that right now. We're interested in a Doctor Malkin. You know him?

AVROM
(*Tries to gain time*)
The Doctor? Doctor Malkin? Eh—if we know him?

INSPECTOR
(*Impatient*)
Well? Do you know him or don't you?

AVROM
Uh, the Doctor, uh . . .

FEIGE
You mean *our* doctor?

AVROM
Him? He's been our doctor . . .

FEIGE
. . . our family doctor . . . for a long time.

AVROM
Not just ours.

Everybody's. Very good.

AVROM

Respected. All over the neighborhood. He receives patients even at night.

FEIGE

He has many patients.

INSPECTOR

Did you see him recently?

AVROM

Recently? You said . . . did we see him recently? Eh . . .

INSPECTOR

Citizen Meirov! I am asking you whether you have seen him—and when?

AVROM

We saw him . . . we saw him . . .

FEIGE
(*Decides to be brave*)

Today.

INSPECTOR

That we know. But when? Morning? Afternoon?

AVROM

Today. Because . . . because . . .

FEIGE

This afternoon. Late. Our daughter . . .

AVROM

Our Lyubichka . . .

FEIGE

. . . is sick, in bed. He came to see her. She's very sick,
but not serious . . .

INSPECTOR

I hope she recovers—but it's the Doctor we're talking
about.

AVROM

The Doctor?

INSPECTOR

What did he say?

FEIGE

Nothing. Nothing special. He came. He left.

AVROM

Yes—he came and left.

FEIGE

He was nice. He told us not to worry. Lyuba will get
better. And . . .

INSPECTOR

Didn't he speak about himself? The situation? The
Jews?

AVROM
(*Frightened*)
Oh, we never discuss politics!

FEIGE
Never! With nobody!

INSPECTOR
How long did he stay?

AVROM
A few minutes . . .

INSPECTOR
How many?

FEIGE
Fifteen. A little more, maybe.

INSPECTOR
And he didn't open his mouth?

FEIGE
He talked about Lyuba.

INSPECTOR
And not about Yom Kippur?

AVROM and FEIGE
(*Together*)
Oh no! Not a word! Nothing!

INSPECTOR
(*Pacing the stage*)
Did he tell you where he was coming from? Or whom he was going to see?

FEIGE
He's our doctor, that's all. He comes when we call him. We don't talk much.

AVROM
We know nothing about him.

FEIGE
We're not his friends . . .

AVROM
No, God forbid!

CHAIRMAN
(*To the* INSPECTOR)
You're frightening them. May I speak with them?

INSPECTOR
(*Sighs*)
Go ahead—but make it quick!

CHAIRMAN
(*Goes closer to the couple*)
Listen to me . . .

AVROM and FEIGE
(*In Yiddish*)
Vos will er fun uns? Zogt eppes, mir beten eich . . . Mir weissen gornisht. Wos will er?

CHAIRMAN
(*Reassuringly*)
Hot nisht kein moire . . . baruikt eich . . . Hot nisht kein moire, zog ich eich. Listen to me. You're imagining all sorts of things. Nobody is accusing you—or the Doctor—of anything. You're not under suspicion, neither is he. He was supposed to come here, and he hasn't arrived, that's all. We are looking for him. Tell us what you know—that may help us. And him.

AVROM
We don't know anything.

FEIGE
We know how to reach him when we need him. He lives . . .

INSPECTOR
Congratulations, dear Chairman! I see they trust you. (*To the* CHAIRMAN) Will you allow me? (*To* FEIGE) Was he happy? Sad? Talkative? Was there anything about him that struck you as being unusual?

FEIGE
Nothing.

145

AVROM
(*Wants to say something, but changes his mind*)
Nothing.

FEIGE

Eh . . .

CHAIRMAN
Don't be afraid! *Ir megt reden! Ir megt ruik reden.*

FEIGE
I thought he was . . .

INSPECTOR

Yes?

AVROM

Peculiar . . .

FEIGE
He was peculiar.

AVROM
To us . . . he seemed peculiar.

CHAIRMAN
Peculiar, peculiar . . . what does that mean?

FEIGE
Unshaven . . . Red eyes . . . Nervous . . .

146

AVROM

Absent-minded . . . like a sleepwalker.

INSPECTOR

And he said nothing?

FEIGE

Nothing that made any sense.

AVROM

We didn't understand . . . talking to himself . . . not
to us.

INSPECTOR

What was he saying?

CHAIRMAN

Try to remember. What was he saying?

FEIGE

He was talking about someone—a shameful person . . .

AVROM

He seemed drunk.

FEIGE

Ill . . . with fever . . .

AVROM

He kept talking, talking.

What else was he talking about? (FEIGE *and* AVROM *look at one another*) Well? Go on!

CHAIRMAN

Go on!

AVROM

He was saying something about . . . guilty people.

INSPECTOR

Think carefully! Repeat every word exactly as he said it!

AVROM

(*Slowly, painfully, regretfully*)
He was saying we are all guilty even if another commits an act in our place . . .

FEIGE

. . . and for our sake.

AVROM

He repeated over and over the same words: There is no way out . . . there is no way out.

FEIGE

No way out.
(AVROM *and* FEIGE *stop short; they realize that they may have said too much*)

POLICE OFFICIAL

And then?

AVROM

He left—uh, yes, he left.

INSPECTOR

Just like that?

AVROM

Without saying goodbye.

FEIGE

He wished Lyuba a quick recovery. Smiled. Stroked her hair. Then he turned to us and said: You are lucky, you know who you are. And left.

AVROM

He went off.

FEIGE

Into the night.

AVROM

Yes, into the night.
(*There is a silence—heavy with foreboding*)

INSPECTOR
(*To the* CHAIRMAN)

What do you think now? You see no connection with the incident?

CHAIRMAN

None. (*Under the* INSPECTOR*'s insistent look, he loses his temper*) None, I tell you.

(*The* INSPECTOR *is shaking his head. The* POLICE OFFICIAL *is smiling. The* CHAIRMAN *is scowling.* AVROM *and* FEIGE *sit down on a bench behind the* RABBI)

INSPECTOR

Who is left? Oh yes, Zalmen! Zalmen the Beadle!
(*From outside we hear the* GUARD*'s voice:* Hey, it's you they're calling! Up! On your feet! Let's go! Steady now! On your feet! ZALMEN *enters, reeling like a drunkard, laughing and crying*)

CHAIRMAN
(*Outraged*)

Zalmen! (*He pounds his fist on the table*) Zalmen, you're drunk!

ZALMEN
(*Turning his head in all directions*)

Zalmen? Who is Zalmen?

CHAIRMAN

You miserable clown! You've been drinking.

ZALMEN

Oh yes. Oy, have I been drinking!

CHAIRMAN
(*With disdain*)

You're a *shikker*. You ought to be ashamed.

ZALMEN

Ashamed? Sure, Zalmen is ashamed. But where is he hiding? Zalmen . . . where are youuuu?

(ZALMEN *moves like a blind man, his arms outstretched, groping in the dark. The* POLICE OFFICIAL *and the* INSPECTOR *watch him with amusement.* ALEXEY *looks annoyed, disgusted. His wife seems lost in thought.* MISHA *is fascinated by the drunkard. As for the* RABBI, *he is shaking his head as though saying no to someone, perhaps himself. Throughout all this,* ZALMEN *continues his game. He loses his yarmulke, looks for it on the floor, ends up falling. The* GUARD *helps him up.*)

INSPECTOR

That'll be enough!
(ZALMEN *does not recognize him*)

CHAIRMAN

Zalmen!
(*He picks up a glass of water, goes over and empties it in* ZALMEN*'s face*)

ZALMEN

(*Suddenly he recognizes the* CHAIRMAN *and tries to be dignified*)
Oh, it's you, Comrade Chairman. You've changed. How are you, Comrade Chairman? And how's the Jewish people, Comrade Chairman?

CHAIRMAN

Quiet!
(*The* CHAIRMAN *returns to his seat*)

ZALMEN

At your service, Comrade Chairman. (*He hesitates*)
What are you doing here? And you, Rabbi? All these
people? Why are they looking at Zalmen—what did Zalmen do?

INSPECTOR
(*Leads him to a chair, makes him sit down*)
Poor little beadle—the most famous beadle in the re-
gion . . .

ZALMEN
(*Contrite*)
I've been drinking . . . and it wasn't tea . . . (*He
recognizes the* INSPECTOR) Oh, Comrade Inspector, I
didn't say good evening. Good evening, Comrade Inspector. How are you?

INSPECTOR
Very well, thank you.

ZALMEN
Oh! Where is my head? Did I offer you some tea?

INSPECTOR
No, you did not.

ZALMEN
I'm sorry . . . Zalmen is sorry . . .

INSPECTOR
(*Almost whispering*)
Tell it all, Zalmen! Yom Kippur—remember? *Kol*

Nidre, Zalmen—remember? How did you like the speech?

ZALMEN

The speech, the speech . . . Oh, *that* speech . . .

INSPECTOR

You knew about it beforehand . . . ?

ZALMEN

Me? I know nothing. I myself am nothing.

INSPECTOR

But Zalmen knew . . .

ZALMEN

Naturally—who else would know?

INSPECTOR

Who else? Anyone. Zalmen's friends. Or the Rabbi's.

ZALMEN
(Dreaming, remembering)
Yom Kippur eve? Those faces—all those faces. The Rabbi growing taller and taller. What a spectacle! And Zalmen, the beadle, hiding from his own shadow, laughing and crying at the same time and for the same reason. What a farce, what a miracle. Zalmen never felt such agony, such joy! *(Gesticulating, he whirls around the table and ends up before the* RABBI. *Abruptly his tone changes)* Why, but why did you climb so high, and why, why couldn't I follow you? Why didn't you tell me that I couldn't go with you? I pushed you into madness and

153

stayed behind. Why? Why didn't I add my cry to yours? Is that how I betrayed you, Rabbi? I want to repent, Rabbi. I want to suffer . . . like you and more than you! I am responsible . . . (*Sobered, he now finds himself in front of the* INSPECTOR—*he straightens up*) But what am I doing here? What am I saying?

INSPECTOR

That's just what I was wondering . . .

ZALMEN

Zalmen, Zalmen . . . are you listening? Tell me what you hear. Tell me what I am saying. Tell me what happened last night.

INSPECTOR

Yes, what happened?

ZALMEN

Nothing. Nothing happened. On Yom Kippur, everything takes place up there, in heaven. Not here below.

INSPECTOR

Zalmen!

ZALMEN

Man is so weak, so terribly weak . . . Good or bad, whatever he does is worthless.

INSPECTOR

Zalmen!

154

ZALMEN

(*Makes believe he is thinking hard; then he quakes with laughter*)

So you still don't understand! It was Zalmen! *That's* the big secret, *that's* the mysterious truth! The Rabbi is innocent—Zalmen is guilty! The Rabbi knows nothing, he lives in another world! Don't harm him! Take Zalmen! Punish Zalmen.

POLICE OFFICIAL

Beautiful! Just what we needed! Another martyr.

CHAIRMAN

It's hopeless.

ZALMEN

Yes—it's hopeless and that's why I'm crying. But who is laughing? Why am I laughing?

INSPECTOR

You didn't drink enough . . . tea.

ZALMEN

(*Excited again*)

Oh my God—the tea! Would you like some? With sugar?

(ZALMEN *is delirious. He tries to get up to go make tea. The* INSPECTOR, CHAIRMAN *and* GUARD *do their best to control him. But he struggles. Just then the door opens gently. The* DOCTOR *enters without attracting attention.* FEIGE *is the first to notice him. Then all eyes focus on him. The* RABBI *smiles. The* CHAIRMAN *conceals his joy with a half-growl.* MISHA *stands up to get a better look*)

INSPECTOR

Well now, so you did get here! (*To the* POLICE OFFICIAL) It's him. (*To the* DOCTOR) We were worried about you, Doctor Malkin.

DOCTOR
(*Calm*)
I apologize for the delay. I couldn't come earlier.
(*The* DOCTOR, *too, has changed. Unshaven. Crumpled tie. Hoarse*)

INSPECTOR

Didn't you know we were looking for you everywhere?

DOCTOR

An emergency call. A cardiac case.

CHAIRMAN

Didn't I tell you? He is always good for an excuse.

INSPECTOR

A cardiac? What's his name?

DOCTOR

Nikolaievski, Anton Pavlitch.

POLICE OFFICIAL

When?

156

DOCTOR

Early evening. After leaving the Meirovs'.

INSPECTOR

Why didn't you let us know?

DOCTOR

Anton Pavlitch has no telephone and I had no idea that I would have to stay with him so long.

INSPECTOR

Is that the only reason for your lateness?

DOCTOR
(*Reticent*)

The only reason.

POLICE OFFICIAL
(*Sarcastic*)

Naturally.

ZALMEN
(*Rushes to the* DOCTOR *with hand outstretched*)

Ah, here you are . . . I am so glad to see you. You are late. Where were you? What happened to you? Were you drinking too, by any chance?

DOCTOR
(*Kind*)

No, Zalmen. I wasn't drinking. I'm quite sober.

ZALMEN

Me too, me too!

157

INSPECTOR

Zalmen!

CHAIRMAN

They certainly make a fine pair!

INSPECTOR

(*To the* DOCTOR)

We've been talking about you.

DOCTOR

About me?

INSPECTOR

(*Ironic*)

This may come as a surprise to you . . . but you have friends here.

DOCTOR

Friends? Me? Hmmm.

INSPECTOR

One of them fought hard to clear you of all suspicion.

DOCTOR

Do you really believe I'm involved in this . . . whatever it is?

INSPECTOR

Are you?

DOCTOR

I'm sorry, but the answer is no.

158

INSPECTOR
Then—the Rabbi alone is guilty?

DOCTOR
The Rabbi alone is responsible . . . unfortunately.

POLICE OFFICIAL
What did you say?

DOCTOR
Unfortunately . . . I should have been with him.

CHAIRMAN
That's our Doctor . . . always regretting what he hasn't
done!

DOCTOR
(*Ignores interruption*)
I should have thought of it before. It didn't occur to
me. It didn't *even* occur to me.

CHAIRMAN
He must take us all for idiots!

DOCTOR
(*To the* CHAIRMAN)
Your insults no longer bother me.

CHAIRMAN
Because nothing ever bothers you—nothing ever
moves you.

DOCTOR
(*To the* INSPECTOR)
The Rabbi moves me. He was sincere. I wasn't. I only
realized it later.

INSPECTOR
When?

DOCTOR
Yesterday. Today. Too late.

INSPECTOR
Yesterday you met with the Rabbi alone.

DOCTOR
We talked. About myself. My life. My past.

INSPECTOR
Nothing else?

DOCTOR
Only about the past.

INSPECTOR
The ritual confession before *Kol Nidre* . . . is that what
it was?

ZALMEN
(*Emerges from his stupor*)
Kol Nidre? Yom Kippur? I know the truth—let me tell
the truth!

CHAIRMAN

Quiet!

POLICE OFFICIAL

Don't interrupt him!

ZALMEN

You were all taken in! At *Kol Nidre,* everybody thought they were hearing the Rabbi! Zalmen was the Rabbi and the Rabbi was hiding behind Zalmen! (*He climbs on his chair, reliving the event*) Zalmen, the defender of his people—the soul of their silence, the silence of their hope, the dream of their dreams—he was lighting the fire and the fire did not consume him . . .

POLICE OFFICIAL
(*Angry*)

Get him out of here!
(*The* SECRETARY *alerts the* GUARD. *The* CHAIRMAN *and the* INSPECTOR *lend him a hand.* ZALMEN, *keeps shouting as he is pushed toward the exit*)

ZALMEN

Zalmen was alone—alone against everyone, alone for everyone. Like Abraham was alone. Like Isaac was alone. Like Jacob was alone. Zalmen saw them—yes, he saw them, as you see me . . .
(ZALMEN *is pushed out*)

INSPECTOR

Where were we?

DOCTOR

At *Kol Nidre* . . . If I were not who I am, if I had a
memory other than my own, I might have waited for the
end of the sermon or of services. Then, like the Jewish
child I never was, I might have stepped forward to the
Rabbi to ask . . . to ask forgiveness. (*The* CHAIRMAN *tries
to interrupt, but is ignored*) I would have said: I ask you to
forgive me. I don't know whether I deserve it—or even
whether I deserve to ask. All I know is that you deserve
to *be* asked. (*He pauses, smiling at some secret thought*) Do
you know what I did today?

INSPECTOR

You just told us—the synagogue, patients.

DOCTOR

After the synagogue but before the patients.

CHAIRMAN
(*Grumbles*)

Probably nothing. As usual.

POLICE OFFICIAL
(*To the* CHAIRMAN)

Quiet!

DOCTOR

And do you want to know the real reason I was late?
You are going to laugh. I tried to accomplish the impossible . . . move backward in time . . . change the past. To
associate myself with the Rabbi—how shall I put it?—
retroactively. (*He pauses*) It was childish, silly of me.

Absurd. I know it now and I knew it then. But I did it just the same.

INSPECTOR

Can't any one of you speak clearly? At least *you* be specific.

DOCTOR

I went to meet those actors . . .

INSPECTOR

(*After a tense pause*)

When?

DOCTOR

In the early evening. Before I went to see Lyuba.

INSPECTOR

Where?

DOCTOR

I went to their hotel. I thought I would find them there. I wanted to see them again. To speak to them. Heart to heart. To tell them—tell them everything. Make them understand. You see, a peculiar idea crossed my mind—that surely they must think the Rabbi mad. That's why I wanted to meet them again. To convince them that the Rabbi—our Rabbi—is sane . . . saner than all of us. Only I came too late.

INSPECTOR

Naturally. They left at dusk—as soon as Yom Kippur was over.

163

DOCTOR

I didn't know that.

CHAIRMAN

A fine excuse.

DOCTOR

I didn't know, I tell you.

INSPECTOR

You were lucky.

CHAIRMAN
(*To the* INSPECTOR)

He's a liar! (*To the* DOCTOR) Why did you wait so long? After all, you could have won your certificate for heroism by approaching them right here in the synagogue!

DOCTOR

I didn't think they would leave so soon. There was no way I could have known that . . . foreseen that.

CHAIRMAN
(*Roars*)

Yes—I tell you. Yes! You did foresee it! You went to the hotel because you hoped—you knew—they would be gone!

DOCTOR
(*In distress*)

It's possible . . . I don't know. I don't know any more. I hope you are wrong. (*He stares at the* CHAIRMAN *intently*)

But why are you so anxious to deprive me of this hope?

CHAIRMAN

Because I dislike everything that is false—false Messiahs, false prophets, false martyrs, false rebels. They are concerned only with themselves!

DOCTOR

I see . . . Maybe you are right. (*He smiles bitterly*) Maybe I did think and wait too long. Too many hours, too many years. But . . . don't you see that I could not have acted otherwise? That I needed first to see clearly in myself? That I had to feel innocent or guilty but not both at the same time? (*He pauses*) But you're right: I was concerned only with myself. Although this time I did want to do something. But I failed. And so, all your "worries" and suspicions were quite unfounded.

INSPECTOR

Almost.

DOCTOR

Years of searching, of questioning, of waiting—reduced to nothing. To laughter.

INSPECTOR

You're lucky. Things could have turned out differently.

POLICE OFFICIAL
(*To the* INSPECTOR)

Let's call the next witness.

INSPECTOR
(*Looks through his files*)
There are no more.

POLICE OFFICIAL
Really? This is the end of the parade?

INSPECTOR
We've heard them all. Here's the list. (*The* POLICE
OFFICIAL *takes the list but does not look at it*) Only those
who were in direct contact with the Rabbi were called.

POLICE OFFICIAL
So—that's it. No more surprise martyrs? No more
saints? Not even a little one? (*He stretches with nonchalance*)
Good—time to go home. (*He rises; so does the* INSPECTOR)
You don't need me any more. This late hour reminds me
of the good old days . . . of my youth. Those long, long
night interrogations. All that's gone now.

INSPECTOR
At least you didn't have mystics to cope with . . . then.

POLICE OFFICIAL
We did—but of a different type. Though in the final
analysis they're all alike. Fanatics are all the same: only
in politics they're worse. Then, too, our methods have
changed. Yours are rather entertaining, but not very
efficient.

INSPECTOR
(*Timidly*)
Our objectives are no longer the same.

POLICE OFFICIAL
You're telling *me*, you're telling *me*, young man.

INSPECTOR
(*Less and less secure*)
My instructions were clear, unmistakable . . .

POLICE OFFICIAL
Yes, yes, of course . . .
(*The* POLICE OFFICIAL *starts to leave, followed by the*
INSPECTOR. *All the witnesses stand*)

INSPECTOR
You think we are wrong? Do you suspect these people?

POLICE OFFICIAL
(*Stops and stares at him coldly*)
I suspect the whole world. That's my job, you see.
(*Reassuringly*) But don't lose any sleep over this. This
pertains to your Ministry—not ours. And you're covered
by your instructions. That's all that matters.

INSPECTOR
I don't know how to thank you . . .

POLICE OFFICIAL
Don't bother. Goodbye, young man. And good luck.
You may need it some day, like all of us.
(*The* POLICE OFFICIAL *leaves. The* INSPECTOR
watches through the half-opened door and does not seem to
notice ZALMEN *returning to the stage*)

INSPECTOR

(*Returns to the table, thumbs through the files and speaks with authority*)

All right, the hearing is adjourned. We are ready to forget the entire incident—if you do the same. Bury it. If anyone speaks of it—don't listen. Erase it from your memory, from your vocabulary. Follow my advice and all will go well. If not . . . Well, good night. And—a happy new year.

> (*The witnesses are in a daze—they do not believe their ears. Are they free to go? The* SECRETARY *is the first to leave. Then* NINA *pulls herself together*)

NINA

(*To the* INSPECTOR)

And—my father? What's going to happen to him? He's so old . . . so weak . . . and so alone. So terribly alone . . .

> (*The* INSPECTOR *remains silent*)

CHAIRMAN

What are you going to do with the Rabbi? Remove him? Ask him to resign? Or . . . what? (*The* INSPECTOR, *busy with his files, still does not answer*) Comrade Inspector . . . the Rabbi? What are you going to do with the Rabbi?

> (*The* RABBI *remains motionless. Distant. As though determined not to take part ever again in anyone else's life. He has seen and heard everything. The* INSPECTOR *studies him a moment, before addressing him in a deep, warm voice*)

168

INSPECTOR

Poor hero, poor dreamer. You have lost and I feel sorry for you; you have fought for nothing. Your offering was not accepted. Worse—it wasn't even noticed. (*He shakes his head*) How could you have been so naïve? Did you really—really—believe that your gesture would shake the earth? Mankind has other worries. Were you counting on the intellectuals? They love ideas, not people. The Christians? Only eternity interests them: theirs and yours. The Jews—your own brothers? In your imagination you saw them marching in the streets of Paris, London, New York, and Jerusalem, shouting that you here are not alone? You thought their anger would explode and shatter human conscience? Well—it's too bad. Your Jews have their own concerns, their own excuses and—who knows?—they may even be the *same* excuses. When, all over Europe, your people were being exterminated, how many Jews took part in how many demonstrations in how many communities to protest, to shout, to weep—yes, simply to weep? Day after day, night after night, hundreds and thousands were disappearing into mass graves or burning to cinders. All of this was known to the free world, and yet . . . holidays were celebrated; charity balls and dinners were organized; people went to concerts, to the theater—perhaps to see and enjoy the very actors you were anxious to reach. Everything went on as if nothing were happening. And today? Life goes on. And those who don't suffer refuse to hear about suffering—and particularly about Jewish suffering. (*The witnesses listen aghast, their heads bowed. NINA puts her arm around MISHA's shoulders. The RABBI breathes with difficulty*) That is why I pity you. You were beaten from the start, you never had a chance. And now you know it. You know that you cannot count on anyone and, what's more, that you don't count for anyone. (*He straightens up. The* RABBI *has not stirred. There is a long pause*) Why should we punish you? As far as we're concerned—as far as the outside world is concerned—you have done nothing. Your dream was the dream of a madman. Why should we make you into a martyr? Turn you into an example? Your revolt, that supreme and exalting gesture which, for you, was meant to bring together and justify the suppressed agonies and hopes of an entire lifetime, of an entire generation perhaps—well, my sad hero, that revolt quite simply *did not take place!*

DOCTOR

You're more cruel than I thought.

INSPECTOR

Maybe, but you—you think too much.
(*The* RABBI, *shattered, wants to say something but his words are choking him. The* INSPECTOR *leaves with a vague motion toward the witnesses. He stops at the door, as though remembering something important*)

INSPECTOR

Zalmen!

ZALMEN

Yes?

INSPECTOR

Take good care of your Rabbi! You hear?
(ZALMEN *nods yes, yes. The* INSPECTOR *leaves. The* RABBI *sinks deeper into his chair.* NINA *is crying softly.*

MISHA *wants to run to his grandfather but* ALEXEY *keeps him back firmly*)

ALEXEY

Come on, son. It's time to go home. (MISHA *looks with distress at his grandfather, then at his mother in tears*) Come on, Misha. Your mother is waiting.

(MISHA *seems unable to move. We sense that this moment will never quite leave him*)

DOCTOR

(*Facing the* RABBI)

After all, what counts is not to forget—isn't that so, Rabbi? Not to forget . . .

(*The* DOCTOR *leaves, backing away. The Councillors timidly pay their respects to the* RABBI *and leave looking guilty*)

CHAIRMAN

Goodbye, Rabbi. And don't forget—Succoth will be here in three days . . .

SRUL

Then Simchath Torah . . .

CHAIRMAN

We'll celebrate the Torah, Rabbi.

MOTKE

Yes . . .

CHAIRMAN

Yes, we will . . . (*To* ZALMEN) And you, you . . . look
after the Rabbi—you hear me?

(*The* CHAIRMAN *exits*)

ZALMEN

Dawn is breaking, Rabbi, it will soon be morning.
It is time for prayer. (*The* RABBI *does not react, does not
move*) Will you forgive me, Rabbi? Can you? Who
gave me the right to push you into madness? Was it
wrong? A sin perhaps? Did it ever take place? (ZAL-
MEN *goes to sit down in a corner; he is mumbling inaudi-
bly. A prayer? Kaddish perhaps? As at the beginning, the*
RABBI *is the personification of despair. From a distance we
hear the angry voice of* ALEXEY: Misha, come back!
Come back, Mishaaa! *Dawn filters into the room and
drives out the phantoms.* ZALMEN, *too, has aged. He is
meditating. Is he going to speak? What is there for him to
add? Everything has been said and nothing has happened.
As at the beginning, he suddenly turns toward the audience,
scanning it with dark, wild eyes, then he bursts into laughter*) And you believed me! You really believed
me! That story I just told you . . . it never really happened . . . it couldn't ever have happened. Never!
Not here! Not now!

(*And* ZALMEN, *the mad beadle, throws back his head,
laughing. And his laughter, like the light, goes dying off
into the distance, among the ghosts, among the shadows*)

THE END

About the Author

ELIE WIESEL was born in 1928 in the town of Sighet in Transylvania. He was still a child when he was taken from his home and sent to Auschwitz and Buchenwald. After the war he was brought to Paris, where he studied at the Sorbonne. He has been an American citizen for some years, and he and his wife and family live in New York City. Besides writing and lecturing, he teaches at City College, where he holds the position of Distinguished Professor of Jewish Studies.